THE FLOWERING
HEDGEROW

Quentin S. Crisp was born in 1972, in North Devon, U.K. He studied Japanese at Durham University and graduated in 2000. He has had fiction published by Tartarus Press, PS Publishing, Eibonvale Press and others. He currently resides in Welling, and is editor for Chômu Press.

QUENTIN S. CRISP

THE FLOWERING HEDGEROW

ISBN: 978-1-64525-034-0

For Mum.

Always there.

Contents

THE FLOWERING HEDGEROW

2ⁿᵈ February, 2016

I opened the bathroom window in the morning and air streamed in with that particular chill freshness that comes just before or in early spring. I wish I had an exact word for it. It is one of those experiences in life that are distinct, but repeated, usually to be forgotten until they are experienced again. Not only that, it is something like an objective blast, in understated form, of the joy of life itself.

So far this year, the air has mainly just been chill, but today, for the first time, I was conscious of this other quality. What is it?

I have been playing Bowie a lot recently, and, in particular, *Outside*. For some reason, a line came into my head from 'The Heart's Filthy Lesson': "These cerulean skies." The sky outside was, indeed, blue. Maybe the experience could be called, 'a cerulean draft' or 'a cerulean breeze' depending on whether you're indoors or outdoors.

I went for a walk at about five o'clock, as the sun was declining. On the way back, I stopped on the bridge over the railway tracks—the one nearer the station. I looked away from the station to the avenue of leafless trees either side of the track, estuaries of branches against a lucid, blue sky. Now and then, tiny black silhouettes of birds glided in the space between the rows of trees. They converged on a faint, brownish-golden colour. The branches were almost the colour of burnt matches, but perhaps closer to grey than black. Unlike matches, they were not dead. Though leafless, they were alive, and very much gave me the impression of life, as if they veined the sky itself. They also gave a sense of depth and accumulation—branches upon branches upon branches.

I have seen this before—not just in this place. It is a sight that fills me with a sense of the lucid aliveness of the present. Usually, however—perhaps always—I can't help taking it also as a promise. I had this feeling again today.

What do those branches, against that clear sky, promise? Will the promise ever come true?

6th February, 2016

It is a Saturday evening. Earlier I felt the need, as I sometimes do, to be alone at home, without communication from outside. Sometimes this gives me a feeling of warmth and safety.

I went for a walk while it was still light. I had put on my hat—the one that Mark gave me. I believe it's a fedora. I had no need to put it on, in fact, and, because the wind was so strong, spent almost the entire walk with it in my hand.

I hoped I would enjoy peace when I got back inside, but there was a phone call. Now I have settled down to read and write. I read Jack Raglin's article on Enoch Bolles and was about to put some music on and transcribe a dream when I heard the wind blowing outside. A strong wind. A good wind. I didn't put on the music; I listened. What did it sound like? A concertina? No—like a train whistle. Like a train whistle from an old black and white film.

A line from the Bolles article runs: "Bolles also began to work on paintings of several family members, remarking that after more than half a century of experience he was just beginning to learn about painting."

Then it says, "A man whose remarkable memory was undimmed by the decades, on one occasion he and his grandson Jack were hiking to a fishing spot in the back hills of New Jersey when Bolles diverted them off their path to a lone cabin in the woods. He approached an aged black man sitting in a rocker on the porch and introduced himself. It turned out the two were boyhood friends some 70 years earlier. They spent the next hour speaking as if a day hadn't passed since they last saw one another."[1]

To find that cabin in the woods—that is the important thing. It'll happen quietly, as if by accident.

---

1 Raglin, Jack (2004). 'Beauty by Design: The Art of Enoch Bolles', *Illustration Magazine*, Vol. 3, Issue 9, p. 30.

It was just after three when I went out to post some letters. The sun was already low, its rays slanting in a cold dazzle on the pavements in front of me. The cold seemed to splash—the light and the wind forming a single impression.

On Thursday, the 4th, when I came back from Richmond, there was a package waiting for me, leaning against the door. A letter was in the hallway—a bank statement. Before putting it through my door, the postman had written on the envelope, "Packet outside door."

On Sunday night, in bed, Bee-chan and I heard a long rumble of thunder, more than once. I wanted us to have a fire, to be able to look out at the rain from a cave, or a tent, or a cabin.

21ˢᵗ February, 2016

After last night's party and a vegetarian cooked breakfast at the Wetherspoon's pub opposite Tooting Broadway Station, I made my way back home exhausted and hungover. At Denmark Hill, I got on the Dartford train. I attempted to read, but was too sleepy. Instead, I looked out the window and intermittently closed my eyes with my head back against the headrest.

There are some occasions in life when it feels like I truly do not care about anything. No doubt, if I suddenly heard news that concerned me, I would immediately care again, but for a while it seems that I am free of care. It is a feeling of sweet emptiness. Rare and fleeting. Always to have to care about personal responsibilities and every cruelty, sorrow and injustice in the world strikes me—when I consider the few and ephemeral moments of being carefree—as a monstrous tyranny.

On that train, before I dropped into sleep and as I rose again to consciousness, I saw bare branches of trees flash by in the clear air, the streets of houses where unknown lives made their lairs, the ugly construction projects about which nothing can be done. Such sweet emptiness. No worries. No cares.

22nd February, 2016

Just drew back the living room curtain. Not 'clouds in the sky' but the sky one grey-white smudge of cloud. Such skies make me feel warm.

I noticed a few spots of rain on the window, though no rain was falling.

23rd February, 2016

Days pass.

Sunlight, this morning, on the fake hardwood floor. Sometimes it seems the cold is interminable. Other times, that summer no sooner ended than it returned, with nothing that might properly be called winter to form an interval.

Almost every day, and sometimes more than once, I take a stick of incense from its box, put it in a holder and light it.

The box is a deep, serge blue (I don't know if 'serge blue' is actually a colour) and there are silver ideograms on the front that say, "Higashiyama. Ginkakuji." Above them is a silver ensô.

Bee-chan bought me this box of incense at Ginkakuji in the temple shop and for some time I did not want to unwrap it. Eventually, I did, after taking photographs of it wrapped up.

Inside is a sheet of orange paper, with enigmatic line emblems on it, and this is folded around the incense.

The sticks of incense are all incense, that is, there is no stick protruding from the burnable incense—it is all burnable. They are almost the same blue as the box itself. The sticks lie on top of each other like a pile of very thin logs. I wonder how many I have used so far. The immediate first impression they give to the eye is still that they are innumerable, beyond counting. This impression will disappear even before it is possible to count them at a glance. Used up, day by day, they must run out. In the same way, the days of my life, themselves, will come to the last and disappear, simply, surely.

"Av it, Nick, you absolute beast!"

I think that is the exact wording of a comment under a documentary on YouTube, the link to which was sent to me by Dominika recently. Beneath that comment is another, in a similar tone of approval, which says something like, "I wonder if Nick Papadimitriou is a beautiful autistic person."

The documentary is called *The London Perambulator*, and it is about Nick Papadimitriou, whose reason for living, or method of sustaining meaning in his life, appears to be walking around parts of urban and suburban London that are generally considered unremarkable and yet which harbour subtle idiosyncrasies. He calls this kind of exploration 'deep topography'.

Watching the documentary, I was reminded of many of my own preoccupations, especially the way that a particular place is also always a particular time. More and more, I seem to need to mine details of the quotidian for a sense of mystical meaning—hence this notebook, begun before I had watched the documentary.

It occurred to me that, with the emphasis slightly more, in this notebook, on the details of time (a phrase from Ernst Junger?) than of place, maybe I could characterise it by adapting the phrase 'deep topography' accordingly. 'Deep chronology'? That seems not quite right, as chronology is about ordering a sequence. There must be something, though.

"Av it, Nick, you absolute beast."

Laurels are bestowed with this phrase. Nick has been in prison for arson, appears to be single (perhaps I'm wrong), and pursues goals that have little or no economic value. He creates his own meaning outside of the economic and sexual arenas, outside of time-honoured religion, outside of the academy. This is quite a trick. What is the value of that honour? "Av it, Nick." From outside, using one of the other systems of value, it is impossible to say.

"Av it, Nick, you absolute beast."

"Av it" is like a colloquial, contemporary British version of the Latin greeting, 'Ave'.

Cooking smells can be heartbreaking.

Time moves forward and backward. In the old days we were younger. As the ever-new of the present burns its fuse into the future, we grow older.

It was dark when I stepped out the door, at about six in the evening. The air was cold. I had a no-man's-land feeling. Walking towards Erith Road, I passed China Gaga. Not immediately, but after some yards, so that the event was at first as if detached and arbitrary, the wind brought me, on its gusty cold, a packet of warm, savoury, cooking smells. I felt a chill then, in my heart, such as a withered nonagenarian, almost bloodless, might feel on the eve of his death, remembering a vivid love affair for the first time in decades.

I thought, forlornly and yet with fondness, of the single occasion on which I had eaten at China Gaga—with Bee-chan. I had felt like I was Kafū feeling like he was Bowie feeling like he was Marlon Brando.

It is March, almost spring. We are moving towards, not away from, the summer solstice. Yet it felt like winter, like I-don't-know-when, moving into an ever-deepening cold, an ever-expanding bleakness. Sometimes, a propellor spins and you cannot tell whether it is turning clockwise or anti-clockwise. Such was the strangeness of the evening that, coming out of winter, seemed to be going into it.

I arrived at Barnehurst Station in time to see, from the footbridge nearer the station itself, a train heaving in to the platform. Beyond the station was the blackness of night, and light that must have been London,[1] icy-brittle and distant-bright. On the bridge nearer yet the station—not a footbridge, but a traffic bridge with pavements for pedestrians—I saw figures walking one direction or the other, sad in their singleness and the cold of the night.

Again my heart was pierced.

I turned to walk back home, aware of a loneliness that contained me as the night did, in which I could walk but from which, it seemed, I could not escape.

---

1 It was not London. I was facing the opposite direction.

2nd March, 2016

Fishknife wind.
　Raindrops on glass.
　A stealthy cold across the floor of my flat.

When I walk, the floor feels like ice-cold stone through my socks.

I read a report on the internet. This February, it seems, was the warmest on record. Am I decadent to feel the cold so much, more decadent to feel and enjoy it, since it should be colder? Is it one of many advance signs of the end for the human race?

　But cancer is part of nature, too. If I had cancer and were dying, why shouldn't I wander in the landscape of my cancer as if it were the Lake District?

I have been reading about the poet Arthur Waley calls Po Chü-i. After a brief biography, there follow sixty translated poems. The first begins with the line:

At Ch'ang-an—a full foot of snow.

It is easy to believe, reading of Po Chü-i's life, and dreaming over his poetry, that life was more beautiful then—over a thousand years ago. It is easy to believe, also, that it was crueller. Can there be beauty without cruelty? Perhaps. But Po Chü-i's world had a future, whereas ours might have none. Then again, we are the future of Po Chü-i's world.

I want to think there could have been another way—that there might still be. I am repeating the phrase "sideways in time", which has come to preoccupy me in recent years. If we were able to go back there, we would perhaps not find in the reality what we find in the poetry, though we assume the latter is a promise of the former.

Here is a line from the second of the poems:

The pines and bamboos were all buried
in stillness.

Could we find the path sideways in time starting from some place like that, in reality or in poetry?

8ᵗʰ March, 2016

I met Adriana today, at the café La Roche, on St. Martin's Lane. There was still the sound of a cold—she called it the flu—in her voice. She had been in bed with fever for a week. With fever, and a cat.

I asked her how it had been—wonderful, she said.

I smiled at her answer. That is exactly what I think to myself sometimes: it would be wonderful to be feverish in bed for a week. Not to care. Not to care. For time to pass in a dream. And then I become guilty and think I am fantasising and that perhaps people who really have a fever are suffering quite badly. But Adriana's testimony confirmed that not all who have fevers suffer, and I felt vindicated.

St. Martin-in-the-Fields. Such an evocative place name. I saw there was a vespers service there today. That would have been perfect. Vespers at St. Martin-in-the-Fields. But I didn't go. Anyway, it was expensive.

I notice a kind of satisfaction when I open the airing cupboard door and, without looking, turn the water heater off or on, and, without looking, close the door again. Or when I fill the kettle and turn it on. Or draw the curtains. The theatre of my familiar environment. I am the performer and audience. The play celebrates power—on a small scale—and comfort. Maybe my instinct is that if I have to be mediocre, I can at least be a genius of mediocrity. But if I am my own audience, who am I trying to please, anyway?

A particularly cold day again today. Perhaps because I spent the night at Shrubland Road, where there is central heating, my flat had that unpleasant, seemingly dry coldness to it, that is something like an uncomfortable absence in the sensation it produces. Even after the heater had been on for some time, this did not change—which is unusual—and I put a jumper on.

Some time after five, I went for the usual walk to Bursted Wood. When I emerged from the wood onto the grassy patch of park beyond, I could smell a baking smell. I recognised it, but couldn't name it. Then I decided it was exactly the smell of hot cross buns being toasted—the cinnamon, the hot currants. But where could it be coming from to be so strong? It was quite windy, and yet the aroma was persistent. The nearest houses were at least a hundred yards away, perhaps more.

I looked up at the sky, covered with dirty grey clouds.

19th March, 2016

Hot water is a miracle.

After I came back from my walk and shopping, I went to the toilet. There was a nearly new bar of soap by the hot tap. I washed my hands and the water was just hot enough that it almost hurt, or rather, it did hurt—for a fraction of a second, for long enough to be stimulating. The water heater had been off for some time, but the heat had been retained. It was as if I had summoned this hot element from nowhere. Modern domesticity is made of such miracles. Soap, towels, hot water, cold beer, tea without end. We take it for granted, as if the world has always been this way. As if soap, tea, hot water, towels and so on are the kind of eternal ingredients of human existence that the Ancient Greeks, too, might recognise. That is, as if eternity itself were made of such necessary ingredients.

According to the calendar, Sunday was the first day of spring. Was it also the equinox? I can check. The calendar is a strange thing if the equinox marks the start of the season. Or perhaps that's logical. Nonetheless, the calendar is a strange, abstruse thing.

On Sunday, I met up with Bee-chan near Leicester Square Tube Station, and we spent the day wandering around Central London. We started in Chinatown and walked as far as Lincoln's Inn Fields, then St. Clement Danes, and then back towards Chinatown and on to Old Compton Street.

After we had had lunch in a restaurant in a Chinatown alley, and bought taiyaki elsewhere for a pudding we ate as we walked, we discovered a Chinese bookshop called Guanghwa. Naturally, I wanted to explore.

Bookshops can sometimes be intoxicating for me, and this is especially true of bookshops selling books in Japanese or Mandarin, and, in the latter case, especially if there are also bilingual—Mandarin-English—books, as there were here.

It was one of those shops which has 'more downstairs'. On a landing halfway down the stairs, like a tiny mezzanine floor, were art supplies, including a glass case full of brushes large and small. They were for both painting and calligraphy, I suppose. Anyway, they were traditional Chinese brushes with bamboo handles. It was dizzying for me to see such a panoply. I felt that I was confronted with a world that I did not understand and could not enter, though to understand it and enter it would mean to be at the very heart of refined exoticism, to exist forever among birdsong and blizzards of plum blossoms. This feeling is an ancient one for me—predating even my interest in Japan. I cannot even be sure when I first felt it, though I know I received a Chinese brush and inkstone once as a gift when I was very young.

Why, I wonder, do I feel so injured when confronted with this world? Why do I tell myself to forget it? That I do not have the time or the ability to find my way through that magic portal? I do not know why, but that is what happened again on this occasion. I did, though, allow myself to linger and dream a little.

Bee-chan was beside me and I pointed out some labels to her.

"Water badger hair." Presumably, what the bristles were made of.

"I don't even know what a water badger is," she said.

Nor did I, but beyond that portal of birdsong and swirling plum blossoms, no doubt the world would be teeming with water badgers, and even stranger things.

I looked for some time at the books in the basement. Bee-chan noticed that a class of some kind—calligraphy, perhaps—was about to start in a small, adjoining room. There was so much I wanted to buy and I was so intoxicated that in the end my desires suffocated themselves and I only bought a bilingual version of the *Dao De Jing* and some bookmarks printed with pictures of traditional Chinese beauties—or "Meticulous Ladies Figure", as the writing on the bookmarks had it.

We left. In Lincoln's Inn Fields, I read Bee-chan Kafū's story, 'The Decoration'. The air was chilly, though there was something beautiful about the gentle yellow light of the declining day. With the story over, we sought the warmth of the nearby pub we had seen, Seven Stars, which seemed to have some thematic connection to the Royal Courts of Justice, across the road. We drank whisky and I tried to work out the titles and authors of the western books listed in Chinese on the back of the *Dao De Jing*, while Bee-chan checked, on her phone, whether the books I guessed at were actually among those in the series.

25ʰ March, 2016

London, Victoria Coach Station. Anti-pigeon spikes on top of the pay phones.

I'm afraid that, although my motivation in writing this is to record "the details of time", I will be forced to abuse time in at least one way: I shall not always be able to write of things in chronological order. I shall attempt to write about Good Friday—today—now, and I hope to write about Maundy Thursday—yesterday—later. Later again, I might wish to go further back in time.

From Barnehurst at 12.16, I took a train to Victoria. A group of lads—perhaps three of them[1]—also got on the train at Barnehurst and sat in the same car as me, across the aisle and a little way behind, so that I could not see them, but could hear them very well.

At first, ancient memories, formless as a layer of sediment, made me ill-disposed towards them—memories of school, perhaps, and of having to flinch in fear and

---

1 I am unsure whether there were three or four, but will assume three for the sake of narrative.

hate myself because I seemed to be naturally one to use bookish words and lacked the coordination that would have made me valued on the sports field. But I recognised the reaction and decided it was unnecessary. I had a slight hangover and I was tired. I did not feel like reading or writing. I would look out the window at the passing trees, houses, stations. Then another layer of memories, perhaps as old as the first, perhaps older, began to diffuse a long-dormant sensibility, and I felt a peculiar sense of belonging or attraction. I would listen to their conversation, I decided. It would relax me. I would lay my mind in it as in a hammock.

So I did.

It seemed that, like me, they were bound for Victoria, and even for the coach station. I heard mention of a coach. There would be a long journey, it seemed. I had the impression that perhaps they were going to see a rugby match, but perhaps this was a mistake suggested to me by my own ultimate destination of Cardiff. Anyway, there was a sense, in their conversation, that they were embarking on a small adventure together. It might have been they were going somewhere or doing something for the first time.

"It'll take about five hours."

"I hope you two have got earbuds because I ain't talking to you on the coach."

Banter of that sort.

"It feels like Saturday," one of them said. This was well observed. It felt like a Saturday to me, too. It was truly sunny and warm, I thought, for the very first time this year. Shivelight fell on the platform of the station that we stopped at.[1] I looked at the striated shadows of trees—a marbled effect, moving. Among the shadows there was movement that looked like someone's hands. I looked up. On the bank above the station, someone stood, twirling his hands for some reason. Then he stopped. The train moved on. In someone's back garden a fox scratched itself nonchalantly, like a dog, with its hind leg.

"What are you going to show them on the coach?"

They were talking about their tickets. Like me, they had probably received e-mail tickets, which it seemed they had not printed out.

"If you lose your phone, you're fucked. We gotta make sure we keep our phones safe for the next five days."

"I hate all this technological shit."

I felt a mellow warmth inside me at these last words. I thought of all the people who had triumphantly told me that if I hated technology so much I should stop using the computer that currently made it possible to communicate with them. They certainly had a point— why *did* I waste time communicating with such people? And, in my head, too, I ceased to trouble myself on their account and was merely encouraged to hear such impatience with technology—with not a priggish voice to challenge it in the vicinity—from one so much younger than myself. The advertisers' brainwashing does not work on everyone, it seems.

I began to feel patriotic.

---

1 Falconwood.

At Lewisham Station, an announcement in the train said that the noticeboard on the platform was wrong and the train was bound for Victoria. The stations at which we would stop were listed. The lads took this as an occasion to joke about people who had boarded by mistake dashing off the train before it started moving again. There was nothing witty or even funny, as such, in their verbal play.

"Fuckin' 'ell, let me off! I'm going to Charing Cross!"

I remembered conversations like this with lads I had known—the lack of inhibitions (at least in certain areas) meaning that they would not exercise quality control regarding their humour. Almost anything would pass. This unselfconsciousness, oddly, made the conversation sound contrived, unnatural. It is the illusion of naturalness, perhaps, that the quality control in the head strives for. A novelist would reject the conversation of these lads as too artificial-sounding. I experienced a minor sense of liberation as I listened.

Finally, we pulled into Victoria Station.

I alighted and found my way to the coach station. My intermediate experience of London, before I ever lived there, was largely defined by Victoria Coach Station. It brought back memories, but not enough to cast the strange spell that memory sometimes can. I had a little time before my bus—Megabus—departed, and I phoned Bee-chan. As I did so, a man at the nearby payphones began to scream in a strangled, agonised voice, then he jabbered incomprehensibly (I am not sure whether he was speaking English or not) and began to hit the wall. I wondered if he might even have a medical problem, but, after all, such a scene, by a row of payphones attached to the wall, seemed entirely appropriate to Victoria Coach Station. People who walked past him looked at each other and smirked. I felt uncomfortable and found it hard to concentrate on my conversation with Bee-chan. Eventually, the man stopped hitting the wall, stood up straight, and turned to the phone, as if he could proceed with business now. He had controlled his anguish and frustration—whatever its cause—as best he could.

I boarded the bus and the journey to Wales began. Somehow, as I looked out of the window at London, I felt captivated. We passed the Natural History Museum, and it looked beautiful. I suddenly became lucidly aware of the architecture of each building, the rounded corners of this brick building or that, the echoes of Art Deco in the windows of another. I was fascinated by the shape of each tree. I began to think about space—the three dimensions, that is. Extension. This extension, containing everything around me, is somehow an experience in my own head. Philosophy. Who had first thought about this? Kant did, didn't he? I bet the Greeks did. What about the Japanese? Perhaps not. But maybe. After all, the Buddhist expression 'the six directions' refers to the three dimensions.

A tree passed whose angled branches somehow filled me with patriotism once again. Who can fail to have faith once he has truly seen a tree? The Daoists were great observers. There is a wisdom to be gained in contemplating the very shapes of things. The Dao is visible in them. See how on these trees here, there are different kinds of branch. At a certain point, the branches becomes straighter, more upright, gathered like candelabra.

I thought of another way of describing trees. Sky-reaching spiders with branching legs. Has that been used before?

I noticed, too, how seldom brick is red, at least in this part of London. It is mainly a dirty, greyish kind of yellow or beige. I must remember this for future novels. In fact, the colour of brickwork varies a great deal. The function of literature is to notice such things in order to remind us to be alive.

Kaneko Misuzu wrote a poem about the colours of sea and seagulls. That was well observed, too.

29th March, 2016

Last night, I returned from Wales. I went to the toilet and saw that the bar of soap, next to the left-hand tap of the washbasin, had dried in the few days of my absence, and cracked, as soil does without rain.

I put on my jacket and coat this evening to go out for a walk. I pulled my black beanie out of the pocket of my coat. It was cold and damp. Immediately I smelt that damp—the smell of the Welsh rain. That damp was from the night I walked to Abercrave Inn with Bee-chan, where we had a meal, and especially from the heavier rain when we walked back to the cottage.

The smell of the Welsh rain in my woollen hat brings back a memory of the cottage. All is transience, this smell seems to say, but there is a wisp of goodness threaded into it, like a skein of incense smoke upon the air.

Because Bee-chan missed the bus from Victoria, and had to catch a train instead, I joined her on that train at Cardiff Station. It started to rain after we left Cardiff, like something deepening, a mellow, wordless happiness. At Bridgend Station, we looked out of the window at the rainy platform. A man was carrying an uncovered harp.

✳

Walking in Bursted Wood earlier this evening, once more struggling with the same anxieties. Artificial intelligence will destroy us all. This will happen because of humanity's perverse but increasing self-hatred. Thinking to embody the best of ourselves in artificial intelligence, we will embody the worst, and hand the world over to it. I am not a creature suited to the fast pace at which these changes are happening. I will take a lifetime to perfect the writing of a sentence. Before I am able to write a book of these perfect sentences, there will be no human race left to read them. The wisdom of the trees and grasses in this little wood will be forgotten—for millennia, anyway, or aeons. But even the supposedly immortal artificial intelligence will eventually face the end of the universe. If I face the end of the universe now, slow though I am, I will be ahead of it.

But everything is slipping away. What is this left, like a hook, in my chest? Dissatisfaction. Yes, that's it. That's all I have to deal with, all I have to embrace—this dissatisfaction. If it is a messenger of truth, then it is permanence itself. If it is not, then I have, by discovering its falsity, also discovered that something is permanent. In any case, not words now, but many-petalled subtleties flowering from this dissatisfaction.

31ˢᵗ Mar, 2016

I have been trying to pinpoint the day of a particular memory. One evening, late, as I was coming home, I experienced something that I wanted to record. As usually happens, I didn't have time to do it that night, or the next day, and now so much time has passed I am unsure of the context.

I think it was Sunday, March the 20ᵗʰ—the day I met Bee-chan near Leicester Square Tube Station. I had arrived back at Bexleyheath, alighting at the train station. It must have been around eleven o'clock or later, but the dark still seemed to have a touch of blue about it, softening it, somehow, and giving rise to a strange thoughtfulness in me.

Usually, at Bexleyheath Station, I cross over the footbridge to exit by the ticket gates or side gate on the road nearer the sorting office. This time, however, I did not cross the footbridge, but exited by the gate from the platform at which the train had pulled in. The road sloped upward from this exit to the main road, and to my left as I walked was a wire fence, beyond which were the trees and undergrowth at the top of the embankment above the platform.

I had had a good day, but I was thinking about loneliness. Life is never just one thing. I had recently learnt that Mrs K— had been hospitalised, perhaps partly due to shock after Y—'s suicide, but I, myself, had had a mellow, peaceful time with someone who apparently wanted to spend time with me. Yes, life is various. And it is not, of course, only that one life is different to another. Each life, in itself, must be subject to the disarrangement of variety. And so, as I walked along that embankment, I, too, felt a sudden loneliness, deep and pure—as real and inexplicable as a sudden wind. But why should it be otherwise? Loneliness must blow through our lives as the wind through trees, even though today it is I who find myself comforted and someone else who is bereft. Our variety means uncertainty. We do not know what is to come, except that death will be a part of it, if not the last thing of all.

But when I had almost come to the main road, I found my awareness, from the corner of my eye, hovering over, lingering among, the weeds and litter at the roots of the embankment trees. Ignored, neglected, life continued there—the life of the soil, vegetable life and life of crawling things.

I realise now that I come to it that I have no words to describe or explain the sensation that came over me. The best I can say is that it resembled friendly assurance—I am tempted to say, *complete* assurance. Sometimes, in recent years, this happens to me—in the presence of trees and grass, I suddenly know what faith is, and for some moments I have it. Yes, the trees and the grasses will be destroyed, too, and perhaps sooner rather than later, by one of the dooms, great or trivial, that crowd our future. I knew that, was aware of it, even then, but it did not dim my faith in the slightest. What is it I sense there, that lives in this rooted life, but also beyond it? On a post-it note, the other day, I jotted down a phrase that came to me when I thought of that moment: "the wisdom of weeds—the uncontrolled".

1ˢᵗ April, 2016

Until this last week, I have had the tiny heater on all waking hours, every day. There have been some days recently when I've switched it off for an hour or so. There was encouraging sunlight at the windows this morning.

I have been very oppressed lately—again—by the thought of the end of the world, or, more accurately, of the human race. There seem to be so many immi-nent ends to choose from now, natural or man-made, though mainly man-made. I think C.S. Lewis is right, though; the real question, in contemplating this end, is, do you have faith? Or, to put it another way, is the end of the body also your end? Or, to put it another way, is the end of nature also the end of everything? At this point we might discuss different understandings of the word 'nature'. Nature might exclude the idea of God or be identical with it. According to Lewis, the latter is pantheism, and the problem with pantheism is that you have to concede that any evil is really good, or that God is both good and evil. But I don't see that a transcendent God, existing apart from Nature, is free of this same problem. Lewis uses the example of a painter. The natural universe might be likened to a painting by God the artist. The painting is not the artist, though you might see the artist in the painting. All such analogies about God, however, seem to me to have the same problem: trying to explain the unlimited by the limited, the uncreated by the created. In the above analogy, where did the canvas come from, the brushes, the oil paints? Were they just lying around? If so, they must have been part of a creation for which God was not responsible, but in which he found himself. Maybe the human mind, only having the materials of creation with which to conceive and think, is simply incapable of understanding God. Maybe categories such as transcendent, pantheistic and so on are mere foolishness. I recently learnt the word 'panentheism' and wish to contemplate it, as it seems in accord with my own instincts, enlarging the field of speculation so that the necessity of certain conflicts disappears.

In any case, we come back to the problem of evil. Where does it come from? Ultimately, all things must come from God. For the Christian (and some others), evil is accounted for by free will. I understand the advantages of this view, and even incline towards it. Still, at best this means we can rectify 'evil comes from God' to 'the possibility of evil comes from God'.

On the 28th of March, I left Wales with Bee-chan. Dad drove us to Swansea. We were to depart from the Quadrant bus station, a site that has its own peculiar place in my memories. It looked like it had been renovated since I had last been. I was not sure that I approved. Still, the Quadrant is the Quadrant. There is something eternal about it despite-no-because-of its quotidian nature.

We found the bay from which we were to board our bus. Dad hugged me and then, turning to go, said, "Right, I'll toddle off now." Since his stroke, his pace has become a kind of shuffle. I understood precisely all the nuances of "toddle off"—the years of survival in which the phrase is steeped, the loneliness and the not-loneliness. The phrase was obviously self-consciously chosen. It is even an affectation of sorts. And yet it fitted the situation and the background of the situation so perfectly, it was as natural as the opening of a flower. So, in this very phrase we see the mystery of free will—that something can be deliberate and natural at the same time. So I see God everywhere in such daily things, though some see God nowhere.

At some point after that parting, the image came to me of Dad standing by the car in a Swansea car park. It was a kind of distillation of the years I'd lived with him in Wales. It was utterly real (more than photographically so; I could feel the breezes in it). In *The Tibetan Book of the Dead*, the dying soul is advised he or she will encounter a great sound or a great light, greater than thunder or the light of a thousand suns, and this is nothing other than pure reality. There was nothing dramatic in the car park image, but it seemed to me that it was, in just such a way, pure reality.

Then I thought of all the demonic and angelic images that have come down to us from the religions that formed thousands of years ago. How primitive and incomplete they seemed. Caverns full of demons—what was this compared to the infinite subtlety, detail and reality of the Swansea car park in which my father stood next to the car? How could they have been satisfied with such crude fragments? Not merely satisfied—they were fanatical about them. For the afterlife—it seemed to me—nothing more is needed than the knowledge that the moment in the Swansea car park is eternal. When we die? I do not know, of course, but perhaps it is simply the full realisation of the eternity of the Swansea car park.

It is not static. It is not flat. It lives. There are many mysteries and there is much confusion around even something this simple. For instance, the moment is absolutely real, but if it is frozen it becomes unreal, and that is what a ghost is. If, for instance, I met my father as he was ten years ago, that might be uncanny. (His present self includes that past self and more.) It *might* be uncanny, depending on the circumstances. I must leave the door open. In any case, in order not to be frozen into ghosthood, each moment must die and be reborn endlessly. In other words, reverberation. The moment reverberates in eternity. This is why when we look at, or experience, a moment, we are not simply seeing a flat photograph. Hell and Heaven are merely the under- and overtones of that reverberation. But/so without imagination we would not be able to see even this moment. And so perhaps the primitives were not quite so primitive.[1] The primitive heavens and hells are a close—as if sub-atomic—analysis of the wavelengths of those reverberations. Demons are the bacteria under their microscope.

So, is Swansea car park more real to me than the various kinds of apocalypse I fear lie ahead? That is precisely the question. Do I have that faith?

There was a woodpecker in Bursted Wood today. I also heard and saw it on the 19th of March. Depending on where it pecks, it gives a different tone, as if playing different percussion instruments.

Friday night and Saturday morning with Pete Lavalette in Cardiff (Easter weekend). In the evening, we talked about the *Dao De Jing*. He had lost the translation he

---

1 The following is from 'God in the Dock' by C.S. Lewis: "The man who wishes to speak to the uneducated in English must learn their language. It is not enough that he should abstain from using what he regards as 'hard words'. He must discover empirically what words exist in the language of his audience and what they mean in that language: e.g., that *potential* means not 'possible' but 'power', that *creature* means not 'creature', but 'animal', that *primitive* means 'rude' or 'clumsy', that rude means (often) 'scabrous', 'obscene', that the *Immaculate Conception* (except in the mouths of Roman Catholics) means the 'Virgin Birth'." This reminds me that I am probably using 'primitive' here in a way that is both derogatory and erroneous, though it is now widespread.

liked and bought another one he didn't like so much. On the back of an envelope, I wrote out for him the twelve ideograms with which the *Dao De Jing* begins, and told him the meaning of each individual ideogram. Immediately he saw how fluid it was, how open to interpretation. He came up with the following translation:

> The way that can be taken is not the
>   eternal way.
> The name that can be given is not the
>   eternal name.

Later, he told me that more and more he is becoming "actively unambitious". I believe this is no empty boast. To be happy being unknown—there seems to me nothing so sweet, so admirable. Yet I write. Why? Because obscurity needs contrast to deepen it?

I am not sure that is the only reason.

Last night—or was it the night before?—my phone rang. It was Chris C—. She had phoned me by accident without realising. I could hear her talking to someone, though could not quite follow the conversation. It was as if, for no reason, a hole had opened in the fabric of space, negating the distance that usually separates our lives and keeps them each unknown to the other. I was reminded that her life continues in the vastness of my unknowing, as mine does in hers. There are billions of human lives just continuing in this way. I was reminded, also, of a thought I sometimes have. If the apocalypse comes all at once, it will be like a dolls-house cross-section of all these billions of just-continuing lives. I find that comforting for some reason. Maybe all lives then will be visible to each other, and the barrier between life and death will itself be lifted. Is that barrier the same one that makes us distant to each other?

I feel I must come back to this idea. There is something in it I cannot articulate all at once.

3rd April, 2016

A clear day earlier, sunny but not especially warm.

Bee-chan took a bus at about half past twelve.

I did some writing, but then was distracted by the internet. I feel myself being sucked into it, as if by a hole in the hull of an aeroplane at altitude. The internet has done terrible things to my mind. It must be because I am lonely. Social networking promises much, but delivers only placebos. I am like a rat in a laboratory; I press the pedals with my paw, hoping to be rewarded. A terrible, frantic emptiness grows in me when no reward comes. Eventually something does, some tantalising titbit—just enough to get me to keep pressing the pedals.

I realised the internet would ruin yet another day if I allowed it. I turned the computer off. I would try and give myself over to writing, today, instead. And yet, who am I writing for? Are they not the same people I interact with on the internet, who give me nothing but perplexity? Or the same people I see in real life, who I might care about, or who might care about me, but who feel no essential need, for instance, to fathom 'my artistic vision' or any other such embarrassment;

no need to get to the bottom of my love of Nagai Kafū (if there were a bottom)?

Anyway, I took out the remains of yesterday's dinner, to eat while I continued re-reading *Kafū the Scribbler*. Then I made myself a cup of tea. The air outside was turning blue and rain was beginning to dot the windows. I resumed my reading. This is what life should be like, at least in the absence of any great excitement (which, perhaps, I am now old enough to do without): reading *Kafū the Scribbler* in the evening while a light rain falls. I heard somewhere, too, the chimes of what might have been an ice-cream van, playing 'Yankie Doodle'. On the ceiling were the footsteps of the boy who lives at number 10. I began to feel more peaceful. Thunder rolled across the sky. There was an interval and a flash, and it rolled again. I checked the time. My phone told me it was 7.20 p.m.

6th April, 2016

I meant to have an early morning to get into Richmond office early, but because I needed to wash my hair and shower I was about half an hour later than I had intended. In fact, I decided not to worry about the time and, even when I was ready, I sat with a cup of coffee and read from my book about Baisaō.

It was raining outside, so I was in a good mood— the kind of good mood that even seems to have layers to it. I left the flat without an umbrella, but returned for one. It was a little too wet to walk to the station without one.

The weather has been very mixed today. Still somewhat chilly, but with intermittent sunshine and rain.

As usual, I could not stay in the office building the whole time, and went out, after I'd eaten lunch, to the book shops—Waterstone's and The Open Book. In Waterstone's I looked at *1985* by Anthony Burgess, who had some very interesting observations on *Nineteen Eighty-Four*, and a Penguin edition of the writings of Bashō. I left for the other bookshop, having it in mind to see if the same books were there and if they also had *Vermilion Sands*, by J.G. Ballard.

I stepped into The Open Book out of the chill, gusty weather, and, in the more confined space, was immediately engulfed in warmth and the smell of books in an almost archetypal experience of middlebrow cosiness which, I must say, I enjoyed.

I found an edition of *Vermilion Sands*, but it was not the cover I wanted. For a while I stood and read from an American slave-narrative book whose title I don't remember. I thought of buying that book or one of the others, but something occurred to me that I had not been especially conscious of for a while: part of the art of reading, the real art of it, is treasuring up in one's imagination books that one will read at some point in the future; therefore, these browsing visits to the bookshop are very important, and sometimes refraining from buying books is, in combination with the imagination of buying and reading them someday, a positive contribution to their deeper appreciation. I was very happy with this notion, and it accorded with my strange, layered good mood of the morning.

However, my eye was then caught by a book called *Exotic England*. I picked it up, looked it over, read some passages. I even came close to crying a little here and there. But I was suspicious of it. Why? It was clear what kind of book it was: popular contemporary journalism with good, mainstream distribution. Yet, I had even been tempted to photograph pages with my phone. The outcome of the internal battle was for a while uncertain. I do not know exactly what decided the issue, but in the end I bought it.

My doubts lingered, however.

On my way up Hill Street from The Open Book, I noticed the swirl of pieces of polystyrene packaging along the pavement in place of dust devils. I was not the only one to notice. Two children frolicked past, chorusing, "It's snowing!"

The weather today was varied indeed. I smiled to myself, though perhaps it did not show on my face.

A sinking feeling came over me regarding the book. When I climbed the stairs to the office, I hastily looked up some reviews. What an abject thing to do! Why did I not trust myself to make up my own mind?

I had been overcome by the feeling that re-reading Bashō, for instance, would probably broaden my mind much more than reading a modern journalistic advocacy of multiculturalism. What did I want from *Exotic England*? Comfort? A challenge? How insipid either alternative seemed. Literature is an education, but it does not set out to educate. It educates as listening to music does.

I wonder at the strength of this taboo in my soul against . . . what? I hardly even know how to name it. The topical? That doesn't quite cover it. Yet there is a hint of the truth there, since things become topical by an easy consensus. I think that, somewhere in my heart, there is indeed a potent taboo, against all things untouched either by irony or by a rejection of life. Or maybe that still doesn't cover it. In short, I have my own ideas of what is tasteful. But *are* they my ideas? If so, I can change them as I wish. If not, why subscribe to them? Also, why can't I be untasteful sometimes? I don't have to find something tasteful to allow it in my life. Besides, I might be surprised at what I discover.

I left the office, when it was being locked up, at about six o'clock. It was raining a little. I was going on to a meeting of the writers' group I used to attend, but I had some time and needed to eat. I settled on The Duke and ordered soup of the day, which turned out to be asparagus and watercress, and for the main, grilled bream with warm green beans, potato salad and salsa verde. Before the soup and between courses, I worked on my story *Fractalism*.

The meal was good, but expensive (I thought) at thirteen pounds, considering how insubstantial the portions of the main course turned out to be. I didn't leave a tip.

13th April, 2016

It seems to me, after all, it is not only autumn that deepens; spring deepens, too.

I've had the heater off for most of the day, but at some point I put on my thick, grey jumper.

The more closely I observe, the more it seems that the seasons do not arrive in a steady progression.

The light in the morning was clear and mellow. The window above the kitchen sink, where my plants are, was golden with it. So spring is not just a freshness and a surface stir, but sometimes resonates deeply, tightening those tendons of the soul that are sensitive to mystery.

Between six and seven, I went for my evening walk. The light was just right, that kind of light that seems to set everything off with a soothing glow of purity, so that the world's surfaces become harmonised with areas of deep thought, creating an overall sense of repose, with enough lucidity in it not to fall into drowsiness. The sun glances on the edges of things so that the edges communicate illumination to the whole world. The angle must be perfect for this, it seems, and perhaps it can only happen for an hour a day, or less. It is like the resonance of a wine glass, when a moistened fingertip circles its rim with the correct speed and pressure.

As I was turning into the Erith Road, I began to feel delicate spots of rain. I wondered whether it would begin to pour, as it had when I had started on this same walk the other day. The clouds, though broken, nonetheless looked pregnant with rain.

I passed Pelham Road, on my left. The sun shone there as if the road were an avenue at whose far end was located the sun's earthly throne, to which the sun was descending now, surrounded by its retinue of clouds. It was dazzling. I wanted to look, but had to lower my eyes.

Before Long Lane, I wondered whether to turn back. There were only one or two spots of rain, but I didn't have an umbrella, and if it started to rain heavily, I might be stuck in a bus shelter for some time. However, in the end, I decided to continue. To my left, I saw a gap between houses made golden by the sinking sun, and there the rain became visible in the glow. I was surprised by how much was falling. I couldn't feel it. I checked my leather jacket. It showed barely any signs of being wet. Could I, possibly, be walking by the very edge of the raincloud? I looked about, but could not confirm this.

In fact, no heavier rain came. I entered Bursted Wood and forgot the rain altogether. Perhaps it had, by then, already ceased.

For some reason, a sense of pathos overcame me when I saw the familiar carving of a squirrel on its wooden column. I stood there awhile. The column was cracked. The squirrel's tail was damaged, and there was fungus growing on it.

I began to walk the paths between the trees and became aware of the birdsong, as tranquil and lucid as the light itself. At the far edge of the wood, I stood with my back against a tree and listened for a while, trying to distinguish each individual bird. By the time I left the wood for home, that special quality of the light had gone. As I approached the turning off the Erith Road, I took off my woollen hat for some reason. There was a curious ladybird on it—a yellowy-orange, with white spots. It crawled on my finger. I grew tired of it and flicked it off. It took flight in mid-air, its tiny wings a creamy blur.

It began raining around mid-morning.

I saw the jagged squiggles of quicksilver on my windows and was gladdened, as usual.

I am on my way to meet up with Jeremy, on St. Martin's Lane. I came out to Bexleyheath Station, taking the daytime shortcut through the cemetery. At the station, I took down my umbrella and held it awkwardly as I topped up my Oyster card.

When I shake my umbrella, raindrops fall from it like silver bells. I feel a strange gladness, shaking a rainy umbrella, on such a day, at such a time of year, almost an excitement, as if I have been presented with a posy of flowers tied with ribbons.

I don't really have the proper words to describe the feeling, I realised, but I continue to search for them.

Fleetingly, the idea of a film made in the 1950s, at Pinewood Studios, flashed through my head. I stood on the station platform. Rain fell on the tracks and birds sang. I noticed the birdsong mainly came from the opposite platform, perhaps because there are more trees on that side. I tried to return to the idea of the 1950s film—probably a comedy. The opening titles would end and someone would be driving an open-topped car along a narrow country lane to a vicarage. The music would be light and frivolous, priming us for the idea that merry misadventures were ahead. The camera would take in a flowering hedgerow where the car passed.

Few people are conscious of the settings of things, but settings are deeply important. The flowering hedgerow.

How many times has my heart quivered with this particular atmosphere? Countless times. It seems to go back before I was born. It is subtle and personal, and yet, surely others have felt it too? Why is there no name for it?

Language is still primitive, though that does not prevent it from being beautiful and mysterious.

At some point, suddenly, the rain intensified. The sound of it on the canopy sheltering the platform became more insistent. My inner warmth increased in response. This intensifying rain on a thin roof—this, too, I have known many times. It is always benevolent. It makes me think that this—this thickening of atmosphere, this vague inner gooseflesh—is what most convincingly compels us to go on living, second by second.

I imagined the same intensifying of rain on the roof of a flimsy shelter somewhere else in the world—Thailand, for instance. I would feel the same warm response, the silence tingling between each raindrop.

But I am ready to see what is unique in such moments, too.

Now I am approaching London Bridge Station.

A good, English rainy day.

On top of the smallest of my three bookcases is a small vase I bought in the small onsen resort of Naruko in the north of Japan. I bought it from the souvenir shop where I also bought a towel with "Naruko onsen" written on it.

I had the idea of using the vase to display seasonal plants and flowers. Currently protruding from its mouth are some catkins and some very small kind of cone or burr, both, in fact, attached to the same twig, and both brown and dry. I should be able to look up what kind of tree this specimen came from, but I don't know offhand. I regret my poverty of such lore. Anyway, I scavenged that twig, already fallen, from a path in Bursted Wood months ago, and it has not deteriorated in the least since, so it hardly signifies the changing seasons at all.

Today, as usual, I went to Bursted Wood again. It was about six o'clock when I went, and a little chilly. No rain, little wind—slightly cloudy, if I recall correctly. For the first time in a while it occurred to me to pick something for the vase. Bluebells are beginning to come out in Bursted Wood—both blue (mauve, in fact) and white. I thought, perhaps, I would pick one of these, one of the mauve ones. Then it became quite clear to me that the white ones were prettier and gave a more memorable impression. They were perfect in a way the mauve ones were not. I stepped from the path into the undergrowth in order to look more closely and select one. I was going to take the very finest, the most elegant, one free of blemish and fully realised in its beauty. I found the one—exactly the one. I reached out. My fingers were around its stalk. Then, for some reason, I stopped. I could not take it. I would let it grow and wither here in the wood. I walked away.

Protagoras said man is the measure of all things. But perhaps this is not so.

I met Jeremy on Friday, and, once we had both settled at the table with our drinks (mine, coffee), we spoke of many things. In particular, I remember him telling me again how Jean Genet had come to be a writer—the fascinating story of how chance had brought a volume of Proust to him while he was in prison.

I showed him my copy of *Kafū the Scribbler*, which I have been re-reading. He opened the volume at random. I saw that it was at the translation of excerpts from 'Tidings from Okubo'. The book was open at an acute angle, as if he were just taking a peek, and I saw his eye fall on the page, even as I continued to talk about Kafū, and, after, it seemed, only a second, he said, "Yes, I can see right away it's extremely lyrical and beautiful." He spoke with feeling and immediately wrote down the title and author in his notebook with his purple pen.

I, also, could see something right away—that Jeremy is someone who knows his literature, like someone who has tasted a thousand wines and remembers them all and becomes more sensitive to their flavours and effects with each new wine he tastes. I wanted, then, to be able to relate this small incident to someone, so touched was I by it. But I knew there was barely anyone I could relate it to.

There is something recharging for me in spending time with someone so steeped in literature. Perhaps we still cannot say, on such occasions, what the meaning of life is, but we no longer need to answer the question— we are both, simply, finding meaning in the same thing.

I have been meaning to write something about March the 24th—Maundy Thursday. I was invited to a service at St. Etheldreda, not far from Chancery Lane Tube Station. Drap had invited me, and there were four of us altogether—him, me, Bee-chan and Dan. The church was situated up what appeared to be a cul-de-sac. None of the others were there when I arrived, and it was raining—persistently and yet rather lankly, in typical English fashion, as if the day is simply wet in a general sense without the rain having to make any concerted effort about it. Lank rain—if I may use 'lank' so impressionistically—and pavements as dark with the wet as the suits and overcoats of gentlemen of former times.

I went into the vestibule of the church to make sure of the time when the service started, but rather than wait in the dry I came back out again to the damp, fresh air. After a while, Drap appeared in his long overcoat, just like one of the gentlemen of the old days of whom the weather reminded me. He proceeded at an unhurried pace also out of keeping with the present age. He arrived and we briefly embraced, then stood together in the rain to wait for the other two. Drap, it seems, had got there before me, but, finding no one else there, had walked around the block. Dan arrived in his flowing Russian robes. Bee-chan was late, and we entered without her. She arrived a little after the service had begun and sidled into the pew next to me, looking, I thought, like some English rose out of a British film from the 1950s—it only wanted for her to take off her gloves and put them in her bag to complete this picture, but she wasn't wearing gloves.

I won't describe the service in detail. It was a Latin Mass, with reading in English and some textual commentary from the priest taking the service. The Last Supper came at Passover. There were old Judaic significations to the bread and the wine.

Of the four of us, three were not Catholic. I was too nervous to go up for a blessing when it came to communion. I had done that before, in a different church, had not known how to signal I was not confirmed, and had taken communion by accident. I wanted to avoid such a thing happening again.

Afterwards, we went up the narrow alley nearby to the Old Mitre for a drink.

Simply to be oneself, that is, to believe what one believes, in all good faith, can easily be seen by others in the world as an act of aggression. Beliefs contradict each other and seem irreconcilable. But we must go on holding them. That is, we cannot stop being who we are merely to make others feel they can breathe more easily.

But people, as such, do not contradict each other. They do not, standing on the pavement in the lank rain, contradict anything. At such times, the world demands nothing, gives itself entirely, though we might not notice. There is no tension. I thought of this as I watched the raindrops in the gutter. Nothing was going to happen, the rain created no suspense, but this, itself, was a gift.

20ᵗʰ April, 2016

Flowering nettles—as if wearing necklaces of seashells.

Amidst bluebells, a single daffodil.

Some time after 6.00 p.m., I went to Bursted Wood, as usual.

Earlier today, I had read an article about a scientist—the same one, if I remember correctly, responsible for myxomatosis—predicting the complete demise of the human race within the century. Such things play on my mind terribly, but there is a uselessness to my ruminations on them and my feelings concerning them, a grasping-and-failing, inarticulate inconclusiveness. The ultimate resolution to the human story is weirdly resistant to mental and emotional resolution.

What is it I am really thinking about on such occasions? "What should I do?"—Is that the question? Or is it, "What should I think?" Or, "What should I feel?" Am I morally responsible? Does morality exist? How can it exist in a meaningless universe? If the existence of morality implies there is meaning in the universe, of what am I afraid? Going to hell? But in a meaningful universe, perhaps I deserve it, and I should welcome what is proper to the universe's meaning.

I simply cannot put my thoughts into words. (How ridiculous these people who believe thought is primarily linguistic.)

In any case, what I came to, walking the bare earth between the trees, was what I usually come to when I am tortured by such thoughts: I must simply surrender to death. If we are concerned with eternity, the gateway to eternity is always now, never the future. The line of time leads into the future and therefore always to doom. That is the world. Eternity is something else, always here, and yet always apart from this corrupting forward line we call the world. Hence, the old injunction about being in the world but not of the world.

To save the world is a kind of selfishness. We are not, of course, saving the world. We are afraid that the cultural and spiritual equivalent of our gene pool will evaporate, all its potential forever discontinued. But what do we think this 'world' is that we must save? There is a confusion here and I cannot fathom it at present. I shall have to content myself, for now, with trying to remember my salient feelings and thoughts.

There is, for me, in the contemplation of all my cultural and spiritual strivings becoming nothing, something supremely distressing, but I cannot explain to myself why it is distressing. I thought of the earth again. My body will decay beneath it and I will become nothing. Very well. Since I know this, what do I have to fear? I cannot lose, because I have already lost everything forever. The world will consume me—it is welcome to me. Because I know that the jaws of the earth will close around me, because I consciously assent, I become a sacrifice, and to that extent I feel myself shift into harmony with the world. I notice I am using 'the world' differently now, perhaps because of this harmony. It is no longer a corrupting line, but has become a realm of rooted images growing from dream-soil. Assenting to my death and to my own nothingness, I feel the images grow in their timeless aliveness; because I am nothing, they become everything, as they should be.

I notice, lately, that my inclination towards Daoism is no affectation. I read the *Dao De Jing* as a teenager. I was shocked, appalled, comforted, and I returned to it repeatedly over the years. The *Dao De Jing* and Chuang Tzu, my time spent among trees, my dreams and my reading and my writing—these are my education and my Dao.

The world—now I am returning in usage to the linear world—the world is full of the babble of opinions— the urgent opinions of people who want to save the world. I begin to suspect the noise is toxic. So why do I write? I want to develop something other than opinion. Not fact, as such, but a resource, like a bottomless well of reflective silence. I want for anyone to be able to drink from this well. The water will be pure, free of the infection of opinion. The well must go deep, deep.

How to do this?

It can be done.

大器晚成. "Great vessels are never completed." So says the *Dao De Jing*. And a bottomless well, I suppose, is never fully excavated.

There is a pendulum that must swing, from the silence of the unmanifest to the speech of the manifest.

I remember the pendulum of the old clock in my grandmother's house. As it swung it descended, descended. So, it seems, to me, the swinging of the pendulum I have in mind takes it deeper and deeper into subtlety, profundity, conciliation, life.

All of the above is my very imperfect attempt to capture something of what went through my mind during the walk. I knew, even at the time, that it was likely the flow of ideas and feelings would pass like a wind, beyond recall. Therefore, I wrote something in my little notebook just after I emerged from Bursted Wood into the little park next to it where people walk their dogs. I wrote: "If it's true I can add nothing to the universe, it's also true I can subtract nothing. In the meantime, I live." I was going to add this: "At best, all my accomplishments will not be more than a momentary flowering and fading."

The sky was blue with only cirrus wisps of white cloud, and elsewhere a white gauze of cloud, but the air was still chill enough that after a while I put on my gloves. The placement of tree trunks began to appear to me like a language of signs, highlighted by the sinking sun. I took photographs, but cameras never capture these things.

As well as bluebells, in the wood, I noted white wood anemones in one place.

When I got home, I remembered to look up catkins on the internet. I identified the specimen in the vase on my bookcase as belonging to an alder.

23rd April, 2016

Again, today, to Bursted Wood I walked.

It was overcast and chill. For some reason I did not expect the chill, or I thought, still chill?

I buttoned up my jacket.

After I had entered the wood, it began to rain. I realised I had not brought my umbrella. The rain, too, was unexpected. I thought I might have to take shelter and I wondered for how long.

There is a strange, walled enclosure, like something ruined, and yet like something that has always been only a ruin—I went there and pissed in a corner, since I needed to. But I noticed there was not much protection from the rain there.

I decided to continue my walk and the rain stopped.

I came out of the wood and entered onto the grassy little park next to it. Soon I realised it was no longer overcast or chill. The sun was shining and it was a warm, pleasant day. That, too, was unexpected.

There were cherry trees with white blossoms—a pretty froth beginning to spread on the slender boughs. I took photographs.

✳

No doubt people misunderstand the Dao. No doubt I am not qualified to judge whether they understand or otherwise. On the day of my previous entry, as I returned from Bursted Wood, I saw some ice cream on the pavement, spilt from the cardboard tub from which you are meant to eat directly, and it was emblazoned with stripes of fairground colour. The ice cream itself no longer looked either creamy or icy. It had melted and congealed, so that it was now a yellowy, plasticky sludge, like the vomit of a doll, perhaps. Two transparent plastic spoons were left embedded in it. Someone had dropped the tub and abandoned it where it fell. You could see the event in its brightly coloured remainder, strange against the grey pavement, just as you can see years of wind currents in the shapes of trees. This too, I thought, is the Dao.

26ᵗʰ April, 2016

Bursted Wood. It must have been around seven o'clock when I went there today. The sun was sinking, and with the carpet of bluebells among the trees, the scene struck me as at once sharp and soft, though I am not sure how to explain myself further. Part of the sharpness came from the cold, but part from the clarity of the air and the light. Nonetheless, the light was also gentle and calm, becoming almost a mist, even in its clarity, amidst the blue flowers.

For a fraction of a second I was reminded of something. What? A story I had once conceived and wanted to write—one of those stories with which the imagination is in love. Could it be *Domesday Afternoon*? Among the material I have actually written, that is the closest I can think of. Yet, I had a sense it was something else—something that has escaped me and that always will escape me. I had the idea then of writing a book called *Atmospheres* in which I simply tried to capture such fleeting dreams and memories in a kind of catalogue, especially as they pertained to the atmospheres I would like to reproduce in stories. Perhaps someday I shall begin such a book.

Before going out I had sent the second introduction for *Rule Dementia!* back to Snuggly Books. There was something in it about Bursted Wood that might reveal me as very ignorant, but I decided to leave it in and merely add a footnote. It was to do with trees being cut down in the wood. I had been horrified to see this on more than one occasion. Only after mentioning this in the introduction did I realise it might be coppicing. I had looked up a little information about the practice for the sake of my footnote. Now, as I walked again in the wood, the information I'd looked up came back to me—there appeared to be signs of coppicing everywhere. Mainly, these were the stumps of old tree trunks from which grew slimmer, younger trunks. Just a little information and new things become visible to you in the world.

I thought a great deal, as I walked, about how ignorant I am. I felt peaceful in relation to my ignorance. I thought, for some reason, of someone saying of me, "He has a lot to be humble about" and me responding with equanimity, even with pleasure, "Yes, that's very true."

Along the way I noticed a patch of bluebells by the side of the path in three different colours: blue, white and mauve.

I walked in the grassy park next to the wood a little, then re-entered the wood, as is my custom. I came to an intersection where one slender track crosses another. On all sides, between the trunks of trees, were bluebells. There is something—I remembered, having had the experience before—about bluebell woods that makes one feel the future is here, now, in the present, and, that being the case, all the tension of life disappears, and a beautiful, eerie, vibrant peace begins to show itself in all one sees and thinks about, like the peace of accepting one's own ignorance and being always at the start.

The basil on my kitchen windowsill now has white flowers. More notably, the bacopa (abunda) on the windowsill in the bathroom is beginning to flower again, about which I am very pleased. Some of its stringy tendrils had gone brown a while back, and I cut them away with scissors. I was afraid the plant would wither. There are still some brown leaves, but the plant is showing its vigour by putting forth its white flowers. Even indoors, it seems to know it is springtime.

The bacopa is perhaps my favourite among the plants in my flat. I like the tangled way it sprawls, not at all upright. It keeps reminding me of vague memories—either of actual experience or of imagined experience. The memories concern a particular kind of English home that seems increasingly rare, though elements of it remain fairly common. I think of French windows looking out on unmown lawns on overcast days. I think of heavy wooden tables in kitchens. I think of a kind of untidiness that is not absolute, but merely gives to the general order of the home a natural sense, as they say, of being lived in. I think, in short, of a kind of tatty, dog-eared elegance.

Petals have fallen on the closed lid of an upright piano. There's a tall, narrow cupboard in the kitchen and the door won't shut properly because it's stuffed with all sorts of things. One shelf is full of cardboard boxes of tea, now torn and crooked. There are colourful towels in the bathroom, heavy as Christmas pudding. They smell just a little and feel damp.

I want to reproduce the phenomenon—the feeling—that I have in mind in exact images, but it is very difficult, and for the moment I have to content myself with the above.

One of the boxes of tea, on the tea shelf, anyway, should be English Breakfast.

29th April, 2016

From the window of a train bound for Victoria: hail, or snow?

It's about four o'clock. The sun shines through clouds.

30ᵗʰ April, 2016

The hibiscus on my windowsill is just beginning to flower, for the first time this year. Even indoors, of course, there are seasons. Every autumn the newspapers try to frighten us with stories of spiders seeking warmth in the house.

On the patch of lawn outside the building, cherry trees are in bloom, but the one outside my window is later or feebler than the others, its blooms still scant. Does it lack sunlight there?

For my birthday, Angie sent me a copy of *The Popol Vuh*, or what seems to be a condensed retelling of the stories from that book with commentary and cultural background. The book is by Lewis Spence, and was first published in 1908. Even in his retelling I can sense the strange, solemn power in this mythology, the imagery in it as dense as a neutron star. I contemplated: Is it possible to write mythology now with the compact matryoshka-doll symbolism of the ancient myths? I think we cannot quite go back. Attempts are made, for instance, with something like *One Hundred Years of Solitude*, but this nonetheless becomes a mythopoeic novel, and we are conscious of the author, and the story perhaps would not survive being retold by another. One necessary qualification of the myth is that it needs to survive continued retelling, and an oral tradition is part of the matrix for this, whereas a novel preserves a precise form of words, and the author's name is always on the title page. Nonetheless, the mythological impulse is somewhere at the heart of the novel, and I am attracted to myth, the strangeness of its great tolling bell, and if I could write a pure myth I would. Even if I cannot write one, I can learn from the myths.

On page twenty-five I found the following:

> So they set out for Tulan-Zuiva, or the Seven Caves, and there gods were given unto them, each man, as head of a group of the race, a god. Balam-Quitzé received the god Tohil. Balam-Agab received the god Avilix, and Mahucutah the god Hacavitz. Iqi-Balam received a god, but as he had no family his god is not taken into account in the native mythology.

I was immediately struck by the last sentence, though it has something of the tone of a footnote. That, I thought, is me. I have a god, but it is not taken into account, because . . . the same reason—I do not belong.

When we rely on the summaries of others, we reduce our chances of happening upon such details. They select what they think is important. We must make our own explorations.

Now I ponder on the resounding unsaid. Iqi-Balam—the Tiger of the Moon, apparently.

1ˢᵗ May, 2016

The hibiscus has bloomed overnight, with a single flower. It glowed in the morning light when I got up, a creamy, golden yellow.

The white flesh of the strawberry, beneath the red.

I bought some brown onions in a net and put them, with the garlic, in a bowl on the kitchen counter. One of the onions is sprouting, like a snail coming out of its shell.

Quivering on this page now, the shadow of a twig of the cherry tree outside, trembling in the May breeze.

Recalling a recent walk in Bursted Wood: The carved snail on top of its wooden pillar at the side of the path. The sound of an ice-cream van somewhere playing 'Greensleeves'.

Hackney. Lunchtime.

In the front yards of homes just before Welshpool House, dandelions in flower and in seed, goosegrass,[1] nettles.

I've come to the Broadway to have lunch. I could have had lunch in the Shrubland Road flat, but somehow I needed to get out into the air—see things and walk around. I'm in some kind of greasy spoon and have ordered a 'veggie breakfast'. Through the glass fronting of the shop I can see the street, and a road opposite leading away to a strange building with a green-painted ground floor, red-brick first floor and a peaked roof above. Above this is a pale blue sky in which are a few small clouds, white and motionless.

My lunch/breakfast has come. I'll try and eat it.

. . . I've eaten as much as I can now, I think.

I suppose this is what is called fair weather. It could even be summer. I don't know what the calendar has to say about that. Last night, on my way to Barnehurst Station, some time after eight, I noticed the fading glow

---

1 Galium aparine.

of the blue sky, and something else—a largeness to the air, as if the lid of the sky had finally been taken off, to allow the air below to breathe. Then, changing at New Cross, even as I walked the station platform, I smelt some savoury cooking aroma—I could not quite name it. This is it, I thought, the chill has finally broken.

But today I have a cold coming on and I feel somehow restless and somehow despondent.

This morning I have been looking over the PDF of the Snuggly Books re-release of *Rule Dementia!* I read 'Jellyfish Joe'. I also proofread it recently, but before that, I think it has been many years since I read it. I have certainly changed, in many ways, since I wrote it. And yet, it's also true that I am still working on the same ideas. There is a single, unremarkable line about fractals in 'Jellyfish Joe' that—I now see—contains the germ of the idea for my current story, 'Fractalism'. 'Fractalism' really is developing the ideas of 'Jellyfish Joe'. It is more specific, perhaps better written, and the point of view has changed. Joe, in the older story, the cult leader, really corresponds, conceptually, to Robin in the current story. Joe is the centre and hero of the story; Robin looms from the periphery, a sinister threat. Unless we take this as a mere exploration of different perspectives, it would appear that I have become more conservative, as we are told people do when they get older.

And yet, I am still in sympathy with the figure of Joe, with his intentions, even if his pronouncements now and then make me sigh. Perhaps it is more that my understanding of the world has changed, not that my aims and motivations have.

There is something about the older story, though, that I find admirable in a way that might now be beyond my powers (I am not certain on this score). Amid the clichés, and the contrived strangeness that was far less original than I supposed at the time, there is real inspiration, somehow unsullied, somehow as if from nowhere. What pure inspiration signifies is hard to say, but I would rather my stories had that than anything else.

It occurred to me, as I read, how much this was written with the attitude of throwing a message in a bottle onto the waves of the universe. This was how I always wrote stories. I suppose I still do, but something has changed. I did not feel then that I had anyone to talk to, but I believed in the value and the possibility of real communication. Someone, someday, would find that message in a bottle and the whole world would change. This mental state distilled something, and that distilled something was what I poured into my prose.

Should I feel nostalgic for that time of agonising solitude and hope?

Now, of course, we have Facebook, and what feels like proof that communication is cheap. Someone may find your message in a bottle, but the beaches are littered with these bottles now. It's not romance; it's merely pollution. What, now, does any of it mean?

Neither the solitude nor the hope are pure enough anymore to distil the kind of inspiration that once was possible.

Or, anyway, that, I think, is the impression that makes me despondent today.

Perhaps I am fooling myself, but I feel more and more inclined to consecrate my life to obscurity. We thought, when young, that we could save the world. What selfishness! How simple it would be, instead, to follow my own small, obscure interests, without caring either for fame or for saving the world. The world, anyway, that increasingly I accept will not save me.

9ᵗʰ May, 2016

Light rain today, but warm. I have kept the windows open most of the day.

I've begun to take photographs again recently. Looking at a photograph I took on the 23ʳᵈ of April, I see branches by the edge of the railway footbridge with a number of scraggly yellow leaves, made yellower by the rays of the sinking sun. Today, on the usual walk, as I was crossing the same footbridge, I was struck by contrast as if I had stepped directly from that April day to this. The leaves were full, fresh and green, and there were no more bare-branched trees along the banks either side of the track. It was as if a film of someone dying and decaying had been run at high speed in reverse.

I had not taken my camera today, as the battery is running out, but I took a handful of photographs with my phone instead. From the trunk of a tree an owl had been carved. It was very well done, I thought, and it was for me one of those surprises—meaningless in that they seem to lead to nothing but themselves—that can somehow make a day pleasant. There had been a carved owl in the wood before, but, as mentioned in a poem in a separate book, it had been stolen. The carver had not been discouraged, it seemed; he had simply carved another owl. I took two photographs of it.

Elsewhere, beneath a hawthorn tree, I think, I found a new and especially pretty patch of flowers—bluebells and stitchwort together, forming a dotted galaxy of white and blue. I took five photos there.

Yesterday, when I went to the wood, it was especially the cow parsley I noticed, a great, fragrant stand of it by the edge of the wood, steeping and stewing in the clear evening sunlight. One gets the feeling that the hollow stems of the cow parsley contribute to this odour as much as the flowers. It is not a merely delicate floral scent, but seems to clog pleasantly in the throat and sinuses, like a woodland cordial to be drunk with the nose. It is as if the scent is distilled from the slanting sun and the decaying of leaf litter. It is impossibly winsome, making me think of childhood picnics that could surely not have happened in this doomed and wicked world, but which did happen, and which, being impossible, seem also, somehow, to defy time.

This time, I did take some flowers for my vase to celebrate the season: cow parsley and, from across the road, stitchwort.

The cow parsley gave a puff or two of its musky odour in my flat, bringing to me indescribable thoughts and sensations. If I lean in close, I can still smell it a little today.

On the 7th it was Joe's birthday. We went to the King Edward VII Memorial Park for a picnic. It was certainly picnic weather. Perhaps that picnic, too, like those of my childhood, was impossible, though it happened. Perhaps it is all impossible, though happening, and, in denial, we think of it always as merely possible. Perhaps simply by existing we are defying time.

I think Saturday was the first day this year I went out without a coat, and in the last few days I have not needed to turn on the oil heater.

Sometimes the heat has seemed to me like a kind of fear, like heartbreak, or the knowledge that I am lost. Yesterday I read an article by Ray Scranton—we are many of us, now, it seems, thinking daily about the end of the world. I posted the article at Ligotti Online. Someone responded, "Why is it so hard to just be?"

16th May, 2016

Before Bee-chan went back home yesterday, we went to Bursted Wood. It was a perfect day of mild sunshine.

I mentioned to Bee-chan my desire to write a choose-your-own-adventure type of book. The branching paths in the wood often make me think of those books. "You are at a fork in the path. Will you take the wide, left fork, or the gloomy, overgrown right fork?" Pure living green pleasure of consciousness finding itself at the crossroads that is existence. Timeless afternoons of my youth, spent on my own with Fighting Fantasy gamebooks, or in woodland glades. A different inflection of the same feeling.

I showed Bee-chan the new carved owl. She admired the feathery splinters around its beak. We stopped here, where the sun fell on goosegrass, cow parsley, bluebells and the rough bark of old trees. A spilt ray of sun on a tangle of leaves. The same thrill of peace this always brings, like a glimpse of the eternity of now—like the true self that is described in *The Tibetan Book of the Dead.*

Ah, but, painful as it is to concede, we live in time, and we had to leave that spot.

When we got to Barnehurst Station, we still had about twenty minutes to wait for Bee-chan's train. She had bought some lunch at the local branch of Sainsbury's—Ribena, Hula Hoops and a prawn sandwich. We ended up sharing, though I only had a little of the sandwich.

Bee-chan wanted to sit in the sun at the end of the platform. There was no bench, however. I suggested standing, but Bee-chan sat on the platform itself and I followed suit. This turned out to be a good idea. Through the fabric of my black jeans (now grey), I could feel the warmth of the sun that the platform had absorbed. It had been a long time since I had eaten Hula Hoops. I resisted the Ribena at first, but then, in honour of vague, pleasant memories that were visiting after a long absence, I yielded. Hula Hoops, Ribena, and sun-bathed concrete warming our legs. How simple it is, sometimes, to find perfection. For those minutes there was really nothing else I desired.

I read aloud from the packet of Hula Hoops—the product blurb—discovering that the snack had been invented in 1973. How did it feel to be older than Hula Hoops, Bee-chan asked me. This was a surprisingly difficult question to answer, but eventually I managed to say I was not especially surprised to be older, since I could remember the advent of certain snacks, such as Monster Munch.

Eventually, Bee-chan's train arrived and we parted.

I walked back via Bursted Wood. This was mainly because I needed a piss and the toilet at Barnehurst Station had been locked in a typical display of British stinginess.

After relieving myself, I walked along the shady road that runs between Bursted Wood and the railway line, where the small, earthy car park for dog-walkers is located. I walked on the railway side of the road, but could still smell the cow parsley. Seconds of indescribable bliss stealing by my nostrils on the breeze. In fact, I would like to describe it and feel myself a failure for being incapable. My job as a writer is to transmit to the future exactly what the scent of flowering cow parsley is like. I picture it as powdery, lemonadey pollen sinking down on slanting rays of sunlight, but it is not sweet or exactly sharp like lemonade. There is a hazy coolness to the flavour it conveys. There is even a slight suggestion of poison. A drink made of this might be the most refreshing you have ever drunk, or it might choke you. Rather than sharp, it is chalky, mixing sunlight and shade together in its sap and conveying these to its clouds of white flowers.

I am aware of refraining from mentioning what always occurs to me in the presence of cow parsley—the elderflower cordial that Mum used to make, which was, indeed, like drinking the dappled sun-and-shade of the woodland. I refrain from mentioning it because elderflower and cow parsley seem too similar, and so a comparison is perhaps only confusing.

As I walked past the cow parsley, and past a green signpost for Footpath 39, I was aware of the call, from somewhere, of a wood pigeon.

The lustre of the buttercup.

An overcast day today—pleasantly so. The bluebells are beginning to wither, but will perhaps last a little while longer.

I especially noticed yellow today. I had already noticed the buttercups at the weekend and made a point of looking at them again today. On my way to Bursted Wood, I also noticed some dangling yellow flowers in someone's garden—presumably wisteria, though I should check, as I don't remember wisteria being yellow. And because of the wisteria—I think—I also noticed afresh the yellow-flowered gorse on the banks of the railway footbridge. The combination of flora in a given area is interesting, I mused.

I didn't spend long in Bursted Wood this evening, thinking Bee-chan might be on her way. One of the little paths leading out of the wood descends a shallow bank directly in front of (or behind) a bus shelter, and it was this path by which I exited today.

I thought about the little canisters of laughing gas I had picked up yesterday. I see these silvery little lozenges all over the green spaces of Bexleyheath and I only recently learnt what they are. Of course, I guessed it was some teenage fad. Bee-chan explained it to me when we saw some around a bench in the park adjacent to the wood. Young people these days, she said—perhaps humouring me—don't take real drugs like they used to. Studies, apparently, show a decline among the younger generation in the use of illegal drugs. One explanation is that they spend more time indoors, on the internet.

What kind of musical culture is inspired by laughing gas, I wonder?

Anyway, yesterday, re-entering the wood from the park, I found the path littered with more of the same silver canisters. There were too many for me to pick them up in one go. I took two trips to the nearby bins.

No doubt it will sound sanctimonious, but I really felt, all of a sudden, as if I were tending a shrine. I don't mean that I was scowling at the sacrilege; I am far from persuaded that the shrine even needs me. I am not really sure what I mean, because it was a feeling that came to me unbidden. Perhaps I do begin to feel that time, experience, reflection and so on, are yielding for me a secret, silent harvest. That reminds me of something—I know what it is. I shall look it up and perhaps note down here what it is when I find it.

Recently there are often days when I want to write in this diary—days, that is, when I have thought a great deal and have something to write about—and I don't find the time, and then, it seems, the appropriate time passes, and eventually, perhaps, the thoughts will fade.

One more thought in this entry, though, from among the many I have not written: buttercups.

They now gladden the lawn area by the housing estate—if that is the correct term—at the end of the road. I noticed them at the weekend and thought how wonderful they are. The name has the ring of a commonplace, and I even think they have become a kind of cliché, symbolising what? Carefree childhood days, perhaps. But it is only the name and its associations that tend towards cliché. Look at the flower itself—that is no cliché. It endlessly redeems its own nature, endlessly redeems the associations of that name. Its very petals glisten and shine, eternally pristine.

How can you tire of buttercups? How can you tire of wisteria?

I suppose you might easily tire of me talking about them, though.

It is the human world that is tiring.

23ʳᵈ May, 2016

I retain a great many images, thoughts and sensations from yesterday, and I know that I shall not be able to record even a fraction of them.

With Dan, I ingested LSD. We spent the day together, talking, listening to music, making notes, and, prompted by my bad back and my restlessness, going for a walk that saw us, eventually, getting quite soaked by rain in Bursted Wood.

Apparently, it was World Goth Day. I don't believe our unplanned celebration of the day was inappropriate. Dan complimented me on the cobwebs here and there at the edges of the ceiling and we spoke about spiders. Since I wondered what it is like to be a spider, we spoke of Thomas Nagel, and the conversation proceeded to many other subjects, notably Zoroastrianism and the divinisation of time.

We played, among other things, The Damned, and I was taken with 'Generals'.

Dan was reluctant to go for a walk, but I was afflicted with a restlessness that I identified with my back pain, and my desire to go outside prevailed.

I had suggested, at first, we simply go to the end of the road, but once we had reached the end of the road, I continued to lead us on. I was intoxicated by the clouds, on which Dan was not so keen—the same "battleship grey" he had been used to all his life in this country. Flowers were of more interest to him, he said.

By the time we were approaching Long Lane, Dan remarked that it was practically summer and still the weather was "like this". But, I rejoined, this is precisely what you expect from a British summer—"bruised arbours," I said, not knowing whether or not I was quoting something.

We paused at the railway bridge, where I asked what a particular shrub with yellow flowers was. "It's not gorse, is it?" Dan suggested it might be something like 'broom'. There was gorse, however, nearby—somehow sooty.

And at last we came to Bursted Wood. A few paces after we had entered the wood and I felt the atmosphere magnificently changed since the last time I had been. The atmosphere, the slight touch of rain, had brought out the smell of the earth, and, above all, the fresh, almost-smoky smell of nettles, which seemed to greet us in a single wafting wave. My blood was charged with enthusiasm for the brown earth, the green that sprouted from it, the shaded air that was harboured here. The bursting vegetable aliveness of it all was a vivid and layered satisfaction. I noticed that the bluebells were almost entirely gone now, a few remaining, only, like survivors from a badly defeated army. I might have expected to be saddened by this, since I was reminded so distinctly of the idea of the aftermath of a battle, but, in fact, a strange and spontaneous delight arose in me. The blue was replaced by ever-thickening green. This was no longer a bluebell wood, as it had been for some short weeks; it was now a cow parsley wood. In fact, it was a cow parsley, bramble and goosegrass wood. The sheer tangle of green, layer upon layer, overlaid by the white lace of the cow parsley, was as magnificent as the former galaxies of blue flowers, perhaps more so.

It began to rain more distinctly and we searched for shelter. Stepping through an aperture between ivied concrete walls, we followed a path to a den beneath trees, where benches had been extemporised with slabs of concrete across tree stumps. There was also a white chair with a cracked back, a couple of holly leaves among the dirt on its seat. We chose the benches. Litter of one kind and another was strewn among the leaf mould in a vortex around us, creating a welcoming shrine of decay and undecay, a spiralling palimpsest of the interaction of the human and the natural world.

This place was surprisingly effective as a shelter, or so we thought.

When the rain subsided, we left, making our way through foliage, as it seemed, of almost Peruvian profusion. The parakeets, of course, helped with this illusion. However, the sense of frenzied verdure gave way, as we approached the park, to a more sedate mood. In my notebook, I find the line, "Six green parrots silhouetted against a pewter sky." This line was Dan's.

We strode about the park for a while, at one point towards a tree that reminded me of Percy Bysshe Shelley, much to Dan's incredulity, and then, away from it.

Dan noted later that Shelley had perhaps entered my head because of his mention of Coleridge in connection with this kind of sedately melancholy English landscape.

Also from my notebook:

> "I might regret for the rest of my life that I didn't look at it more." (after Coleridge)

We went to the local Sainsbury's for provisions, these being cookies, crisps, Elderflower Pressé, tonic water and two plastic wine glasses. Then we returned to the wood.

Before we could find the den once more, it began to rain quite heavily. We mistook the way and had to retrace our steps and then to retrace them again. Eventually we did find the way, but it soon became apparent that the idea that this thin canopy had provided shelter before was an illusion. We were quickly becoming soaked. Perhaps there was at least time for a toast, with Elderflower Pressé and tonic. The toast: "To eternal time!"

And then we abandoned our plastic glasses on the white chair and fled. "Fleeing in terror, clutching a Sainsbury's bag," as Dan was to describe me.

It had been quite some time since I'd got that soaked.

I returned to the wood today. The plastic glasses were still on the seat. One toppled, one containing, I suppose, a mix of Elderflower Pressé and tonic, and rain.

This is the last thing that was written, yesterday, in the little yellow notebook whose pages are now a little warped from rain:

> The negative aim of modernity is to persuade one to mistrust oneself.

Yesterday, Camden.

Past the shop's back room and another back room and out into the yard crammed with furniture, most of it, quite possibly, for the scrapheap.

On the table, a *Q* magazine from 2005, the anniversary issue of Lennon's death.

"Over ten years ago now," I say.

"Just old enough to be interesting again. You don't want to read one from two years ago."

On the cover, "pathetic rock stars", and a photo of Morrissey in the corner. This is a source of amusement.

John says he never liked Morrissey much apart from a song here and there.

"'The Last of the Gang . . .'" He searches for the title.

Dan thinks he means 'The Last of the Famous International Playboys'. I know he doesn't.

"'The First of the Gang to Die'," I say.

Dan sings the chorus.

John laughs.

"How does it go again, Dan?"

Tara seems to be saying that she has been a man a few times before. I ask if she gravitates more towards male or female. I suspect the latter. I am not sure she understands my question.

That day, I am sure, I thought of Larkin's 'An Arundel Tomb'.

I am thinking about it a great deal today.

"Only the wounded remain."

Yet we carry on.

29th May, 2016

What I thought was wisteria was probably laburnum.

30th May, 2016

Bank Holiday.

A dull day. Some time in the late morning or afternoon, I looked out the window to see the air dark. The cherry tree outside has long been without blossoms now. The green leaves seemed to emphasise the gloom of the day. I felt a strange, faint gladness.

A wind rose up at some point. It was perhaps eight o'clock by the time I went out for my usual walk, and the weather was blustery. I was aware of a nameless melancholy in my heart. Age? Obscurity? The usual things, perhaps, but melancholy has a way of renewing itself, so that it is forever potent, mysterious, even seductive.

Perhaps the wind had blown away the earlier clouds—presumably so. The sky was clearer than in the afternoon, with only traces of pink cloud remaining, like mother-of-pearl in the patterns of a sandy shoreline.

When I got back, I finished looking over the PDFs Snuggly Books had sent for the re-release of *Rule Dementia!*

I had eaten some leftover pasta before my walk and was not sure whether to supplement this with something now or not. I decided on a crust of bread with Marmite and miso soup to dip it in. I read from Matsumoto Hajime's book about Kafū as I ate. The chapter was on old age. Matsumoto quotes various sections of Kafū's diary related to growing old.

In one entry, written when he was fifty-six, Kafū says that he sat at his desk to write but, listless, leafed through some year-old journals instead, late into the night. The desire to create, he opines, is like sexual desire. It is natural that, even as sexual desire fades with age, so does the desire to make art.

As Matsumoto points out, Kafū was not a spent force yet.

I still feel my best writing must be ahead of me and yet I, too, am aware of a time limit and sometimes wonder if my appetite itself will dry up.

There is no point, perhaps, in siring a child you are too old to rear. And perhaps there is no point in creating art for a world in which, by dint of lack of future, you are no longer interested.

2nd June, 2016

Not a summery start to June.

I have not had the windows open today, as recently. Or rather, I opened the bathroom window in the morning and noticed the cold even in the living room, between two closed doors. I shut the window again and have had the oil heater on all day.

I went for my usual walk to Bursted Wood at perhaps six o'clock. The ground is still muddy from recent rains and the great stands of cow parsley look slightly battered. I am just a little worried that it might already be too late this year for me to drink deeply, with my nostrils, the scent of cow parsley, in order to grasp its essence and put it into words for some godforsaken post-organic generation of the future.

The muddy ground and the dull, cold air brought to my mind, by contrast, the dry paths in sunshine that have been, for me, part of the secret magic of recent days, fermenting in me an image that might, someday, grow into a story.

The dry earth, in quiet sunlight. This, in short, is what we call 'day'. It is a subliminal eternity, an eternity that nonetheless slips away, leaving a pain as if an intravenous tube were suddenly torn from us.

Day is the eternity we do not notice; fear what we feel when we believe it will be lost forever.

In the entry for the 17th of May, I noted that some thoughts of mine reminded me of something. I have tracked that something down. It is part of a Goodreads review, by Bill Kerwin, of Richard Rohr's *Falling Upward*. It goes like this:

> Our task in the first half of life, Rohr tells us, is to construct "the proper container" for our lives and adopt a system of rules that will keep our "container" strong enough to endure the challenges of the early years, all the while permitting the self to flower. First half folks are often obsessed with law, order, custom, tradition, correct rituals, controlling (or refusing to control) passion and pleasure, safety, and intellectual certainty.
>
> Second-half folks who get stuck in first-half tasks—or, like me, in a first-half institution—find it difficult to continue their explorations the way the second half of life requires. For us, it is the tragic sense of life that matters, the sense that growth and redemption spring naturally from inevitable sins and necessary sorrows. It is in this—not in any nit-picky concepts of right and wrong—that we find our

meaning and consolation. The container itself is no longer enough, and we begin to journey toward an ancient self with a new homesickness, to enter into a second simplicity, to accept, with a new inner brightness, the old inescapable sadness.

Beautifully expressed, but I am suddenly unsure how applicable it is in my case. Nonetheless, I feel resonance of some kind here, even if only in that I feel I have very much entered a second half of life, and in that sense a new beginning, though a new beginning defined by its greater proximity to the end.

I can say at least one thing in favour of the seemingly counterintuitive idea that younger people are more obsessed by laws. Youth is known as a time of questioning and rebellion, but, as it appears to me now, the questioning is generally not true—which is to say, not very thorough—questioning. It is usually closer to mere rejection. Perhaps this is a necessary phase, but it would be terrible if this were how things ended. True questioning does not simply reject in order to reinforce an existing identity; it holds the object of questioning close, and the future relationship between the subject and the object of the questioning is suspended in uncertainty. In short, to question—truly to question—one must admit one's ignorance. This is very hard for someone who is determined to rebel.

I am not sure, myself, that I constructed an adequate container during the first half of my life. Instead of a glazed vase holding a hibiscus, I have—to use a rather cheap analogy—a daisy in a rough, unglazed pot. This is often a source of considerable sadness and regret for me. Still, I know how hard I worked on that pot. I see my thumbprint here, my fingerprint there, and recognise the designs that were in my mind. It is something. The depth of my knowledge that this pot is something is precisely what matters now, since that knowledge will help me make the most of whatever meagre flowers I can collect to put in that modest and rather clumsy vessel.

6th June, 2016

Walking along Regent's Canal yesterday, to and from Victoria Park.

On one side, burgeoning white flowers in zesty lances. Are they a kind of buddleia? White profusion? Or are they hebe? I don't know. Now I think of it, I even wonder if they were blackthorn, though the flowers were not grouped in the right way. They had the same sweet-sharp, powdery summer scent.

On the other side of the canal, on the way back, cow parsley and ivy overwhelm the brickwork of a building with something of a warehouse feel to it—a reflection doubles the image.

Ripples cross each other silently.

Sometimes in a life, one stays over somewhere—with a friend, girlfriend, boyfriend, acquaintance—and the person whose guest you are has to leave in the morning, earlier than you. On such occasions, other people's bathrooms and other people's kitchens take on a peculiar significance—I want to say, an existential attraction, but perhaps I am using the term 'existential' so loosely as to be misleading. In any case, I have felt this attraction again and again in my life and have never been able to arrive at a conclusive analysis of it.

The first thing to say, of course, is that you are confronted with another person's domesticity in their absence. But why is the feeling I have in mind so much stronger in relation to bathrooms and kitchens than it is, say, to living rooms? Perhaps I have something like an answer.

In relation to the kitchen, it is the scattered crumbs around the toaster, or the lingering aroma of coffee, or a few items of washing up left in the sink that give this feeling. That is, the feeling comes from the mixed impressions of domestic comfort and the hurried business of life, specifically as experienced from the point of view of a bystander who is thrown a little out of his normal routines. It is the leftovers of breakfast, eaten when one has an eye on the time because of work, that give rise to this feeling, not the leftovers of last night's dinner.

In relation to the bathroom, the impression is perhaps more diffuse, but can be, I think, quite as strong. There are usually things to be done in the bathroom in order to transform oneself from a sleepy domestic creature with tangled hair, to a smart, fresh-smelling citizen of the Land of Office Hours. The shower gel gives off a sharp, brisk scent that seems charged with rush-hour readinesss. Even the towel, hanging from its hook, with friendly patterns of anchor and wave, has a sense in its repose of having been left where it was by someone in danger of missing a train or bus. Alone in the house or flat, you might stand in the doorway of the bathroom for a while, feeling somewhat vacant, looking around and wondering if you'll be able to leave the bathroom as your host habitually leaves it. You might even doubt your ability to use the shower. A nervous tingle comes over you, often strangely pleasant, but sometimes verging on the unpleasant. In the latter case, it includes a sense of unease, the vague, cloying suspicion that you are not doing all you should in order to cope with your life in an adult way. In the former case, it includes a sense that, after all, none of it matters.

It is this reminder, in the tingle, of adult responsibilities, that perhaps holds the key to the entire feeling. The feeling takes me back to student days in the 1990s. First, I would visit friends in their student digs, then, later, I too entered university as a mature student. We were away from home for the first time—though that wasn't strictly true in my case—and enjoying a strange mixture of new responsibility and new irresponsibility. We had to deal now with kitchens and bathrooms of our own, and for a while there was a playacting feel to this, as if we were children trying on our parents' clothes. Kitchens and bathrooms contain the practical things of daily life, and the things that most often need to be restocked. There are rows of herbs, spices, sandwich spreads, in the kitchen cupboards; on the bathroom shelf there stands an array of shampoos, conditioners, mouthwash, eye drops, and more esoteric lotions, liquids, creams and powders. These things denote daily activity, and what needs to be done to sustain daily activity.

I still feel now the mixture of playacting and seriousness with which I became acquainted in those student years. The bathrooms and kitchens seem largely the same now as they were in the nineties, though now, I note, you are more likely to find plastic bottles whose product descriptions inform you that they are a "vegan-suitable lemon and pomegranate zingy morning bracer", or some such thing. Consumption and alternative lifestyles had not fused so entirely yet in the nineties.

On the whole, despite a queasiness around the edges, because you should be somewhere, too, and you also have work to attend to, such mornings, left to your own devices in your host's home, are one of the better things in life. Not quite sure where everything is, you poke through the cupboards, trying to remember what you can and can't eat (if, for instance, your host shares the place with others). Might you use this milk? Is there any decent tea? You manage, after all, to scrape together a breakfast, quite different to what you would normally eat. You look at the periodicals left on the living room table. As you sit down with your mug of tea and your whitecurrant jam on toasted rye bread, you idly pick up the biannual journal of metropolitan canal life, *Waterfront*. It is issue #3. You read an article on the mating habits of herons. It might be pleasant to spend a whole day like this, but you know you have to get back to your own life soon.

8th June, 2016

Yesterday, just before one o'clock in the afternoon, there was thunder, and soon rain was spattering the windows. Today the thunder came a little later. Perhaps it was more like two o'clock.

Why do I like the thunder? It makes me feel as if I am about to be released, though this promise is never fulfilled. To be spent like lightning in a flash, and then for there only to be the peace of falling rain!

When I went to Bursted Wood this evening, it was muddy and I had to tread carefully. Rain and mud got in through the hole in the side of my right shoe. I noted that all the blue flowers of the bluebells are now gone. I could see the plants themselves still—green and naked, as if roughly stripped bare.

When I walked up the bank at the edge of the park area, the air was full of floating downy gossamer—a nearby tree was shedding seeds.

I had been thinking how, if my life ended at this moment, everything I have worked for all these years, with head, heart and hands, would not only be unfinished, but would be without meaning for those left behind. Even those who appreciated would not know the way in which my scheme was tending. I walk among people—sometimes the same people for year after year—and they seem not to suspect I even have a scheme. And, in the end—probably soon—its incompleteness would tend to decay and ruin and it would be forgotten. In short, all would be as if I had never existed and never spent my days in such exertions and anxiety. I felt a ghastly sickness at the thought, and then . . . As always, a split-second realisation that the ghastly sickness is inevitable as long as one lives. I will cease and so will the sickness. How wonderful. I will be free. I will be rid of people forever. And rid of loneliness and fear and the whole wrangle of it all.

After 10 p.m.

I take one path through the wood, unbranching till I come to the carving of the crow, and am reminded how small it really is. How many acres, I wonder? When I first found this wood, I thought it little more than a copse, barely of interest at all, except inasmuch as it gave an overgrown impression to the grass verges at the side of the road. Grass verges—which induce in us a nervous feeling of homelessness when we are on the edge of mental illness, because they highlight how shorn of organic life the world has become, though we are organic in our origins.

Coming out from under the trees into the park. A new moon, strong and yellow. The sky still glows with the summer day, a translucent, almost pearly blue. The trees are silhouettes beneath, verdant with quite particular leafage. Thin clouds form oddly angular streaks and wedges in the sky. There is no easy flow to them, but they are magnificent nonetheless. Two of them might be vapour trails. They grow larger above the nearby tree like the crooked ears of a gigantic hare. The grass in this small park is now redolent of meadow.

The night has a tender and expansive clarity and the nocturnal air should be stirring among the seedy heads of grass like bees among flowers.

I walk back home knowing I must do more work, though having no appetite for it. I think of that sky.

June, I think, is one of the most stressful months of the year for me. I fill in my tax return, after doing my yearly accounts. I apply for the renewal of tax credits. I apply for another deferment of the repayment of my student loan. And it seems there are always deadlines and extra work. I did better than usual with my writing last year, but the money is running out, and I must cast about for editing jobs and publishers who will accept short stories from me. I might work some months on a story that fetches less than what an ordinary person makes in a week.

12th June, 2016

At lunch, yesterday, with Bee-chan and her mother in Oxford. We tried to identify, by my description, the tree mentioned in the entry for the 8th of June, which was shedding downy seeds. With the help of the internet and a couple of old guidebooks to British flora and fauna, we struck upon aspen as a likely candidate.

I went to Bursted Wood at about eight o'clock this evening. It was muddy again, from recent rain. The greenery even looked battered, as if each rainfall that attains any degree of force is a kind of disaster in the vulnerable and yet resilient kingdom of vegetation. I noticed that the white flowers are now almost entirely gone from the cow parsley there.

I got to the tree at the edge of the park from which the downy seeds came. There was more than one, in fact. At least two. I picked one of the catkins, fluffy with down, from one of the trees, and also took a sprig of leaves for identification. I have now put both the catkin and the leaves in the vase atop my bookcase. Checking these leaves against photographs of aspen leaves online serves to confirm what we thought.

The Latin name is *Populus tremula*. Apparently there is an old idiom, "to tremble like an aspen". Folklore suggests the leaves of this tree tremble more readily than those of others because of guilt or fear at having supplied the wood for the cross on which Christ was crucified.[1]

The grass in the park is so long now my shoes become wet and get covered in seeds when I walk through it. There are many different plants and flowers among this grass, clover and daisies being only the most obvious. I particularly notice patches of tiny yellow flowers with stringy stems and leaves. Are these *Sinapis arvensis*? I don't know. I'll need to take a sample, next time, to try and identify it.

Walking through such unruly grasses, I could begin to imagine I was in a warmer climate and a country of more extensive uncultivated spaces than Britain. I thought, for some reason, of the Buddha's birthplace— or is it where he died?—which I was told, by a friend who visited the spot, was nothing but weeds and grasses, without any kind of marker or memorial.

---

1 The information in this paragraph, as with most scholarly information in this diary, represents research in progress and is not intended to be taken as authoritative. I encourage interested readers to do their own research.

13th June, 2016

Anxiety continues.

I received a letter from Npower, my supplier of electricity, this morning. The tone was threatening—"our right to enter your home"—and they were demanding a sum of £106.26 even though I had already paid my bill last month. For some reason, my electricity bills have gone up considerably in the last year. When I contacted Npower about this rise before, they first refused to understand my complaint, then said all bills were based on the meter readings I had sent. I dare say the bills are correct, but I would not know either way if they weren't. Of course, when I phoned today, they merely said they had miscalculated my bill last time. By £106? It seems a huge amount to add. If I only had time to get myself from under the scrabble for mere survival, I might be able to check on these matters in detail. But I don't have time. The external world demands, demands, demands . . . I am lucky to get any time at all for the contemplative solitude I need, let alone to reorganise my life so that I can escape the demands, demands, demands.

I am afraid that I will not defer the repayment of my student loan in time. I made an effort on the paperwork today. I went out to get some money from the cashpoint to pay for printout, as my printer hasn't worked for years. The roads and pavements were wet and it began to rain again—a full, wet rain, promising a downpour at some point. I would get my umbrella on the way back. At least, despite my anxieties, there is this sweet, sweet rain, I thought. When I got to the internet café, the rain attained the heaviness it had threatened. The proprietor gestured outside.

"That's the end of summer for this year," he said. "Just look at it! It's terrible, isn't it?"

Somehow, I could not bring myself to make the conventional response. One grows up taking it for granted that rain is bad, but why does this ludicrous opinion persist? I find it exceedingly strange that people continue to express such sentiments, as if they are quite in earnest. They might as well complain every time the sun sets.

"It doesn't look so bad to me," I managed.

I couldn't remember the password for my e-mail in order to print out the documents I'd e-mailed myself and had to go back to the flat in order to retrieve the little notebook in which I write down my passwords.

It is not only because of stress and financial worry that I feel anxious.

One of the other sources of anxiety might be represented by the short film 'Sunspring', which I watched on YouTube this afternoon. The script was written by an AI that some humans are pretending has asked to be called Benjamin. The current materialist position: humans are not conscious, but machines are. Considering the fact they seem to believe that humans are only machines, anyway, you'd think they would, therefore, concede the existence of human consciousness.

The script, in fact, is gibberish, but is given coherence by the performances of the human actors. Actually, what this amounts to is nothing other than the cut-up technique, as used by William Burroughs, but automated. For some time now I have been disillusioned with the ethos of the cut-up. Bowie, for instance, used it as a means of unleashing creative potential, but I fear the net cultural result might have been only a lowering in standards of songwriting, since now anyone can sound meaningful while having nothing to say. "Stop making sense," David Byrne exhorted us. But sense seems to me to have scarcity value now; gibberish has flooded the market.

Having said that, I don't think that the cut-up is always a bad idea or always unproductive. The problem is that the contemporary attitude seems to be: something is only meaningful if I can't understand what it means.

The cut-up, really, is a form of bibliomancy. We take words at random and assume, for the sake of experiment, that they are oracular. The AI author automates this process at high speed. The bibliomancer opens a book, eyes closed, and puts his finger on the page. All the words in the book he opened came from a living human author. He is finding meaning in the aleatory selection of one word or phrase or line among them. First the words written, with some intention or another, by someone else, then the random selection, then the interpretation of that random selection by the bibliomancer. What we are doing now, as a society, is raising the random part of the process above all the rest, at once finding all meaning in it, denying all meaning through it, and ignoring the existence of the other stages of the process that supplied all the meaning we find in and deny through the randomness.

It is this habit that typifies the utter hatefulness of modernity. Of course, I have been part of this, and suppose I still am to some degree. We long for an alien world, as if only the alien, the incomprehensible, can reveal the truth. We ignore the miracle of comprehensibility in our everyday lives. I already understand the alien language known as 'English'—I am an insider, privy to this mysterious secret, along with a number of others—large or small, depending on perspective—in some far-flung purlieu of the universe that might or might not also be the centre.

People are hateful because they do not appreciate what they have. They destroy the sacred Rubin vase of the ordinary, thinking this will set free the cryptic shadow that it casts. With nothing to cast it, the shadow disappears. Once I understand the alien language, that language becomes merely another English. It is only by appreciating the strangeness in my native language in the first place, that I can hope to appreciate, for any length of time, the strangeness of another language. It is the living, growing, complementary contrast that is important.

Capitalism and technology of the electronic variety have become entwined. This is from 'On the Jewish Question', by Karl Marx:

> Money is the alienated essence of man's labour and life, and this alien essence dominates him as he worships it.

It is easy enough, now, to substitute here "technology" for "money".

I sometimes try bibliomancy myself; I am not necessarily averse to it, though undecided on its value. I strongly suspect, though, that those who make obeisance before what is essentially computerised bibliomancy would see my manual bibliomancy (digital in the original sense of the word) as superstitious rot. This is another indication of the irrational reverence that humans currently have for anything electronic. Whatever elements of the AI are not aleatory or automatic are precisely those elements provided in advance by humans.

I did collect some samples today, as I had intended, from the park by Bursted Wood. I realised, as I searched the grasses, that there was more than one yellow-flowered weed here. My remembered impression was of one such weed, which fused the qualities of at least two species. I am reminded again, as I usually am when I return to check a remembered scene, that one must be suspicious of casual impressions.

I have brought three types of weed back with me to investigate. One of them, though, was from the grass verge between Bursted Wood and the road, rather than from the park itself. After much searching on the internet, I believe the specimens are lesser trefoil, some kind of Oxalis (with very tiny yellow flowers and brownish patches on its leaves), and hedge mustard (the one from the verge).

The investigation on Saturday regarding the trees with downy seeds was brought about by the presence of two gloriously old-fashioned illustrated guidebooks. I should have more such books myself. There is a kind of tranquillity to them.

One of these books was open at the pages (textual verso and illustrated recto) for bats. There seemed something felicitous in this (bibliomancy, if you fancy). A bat features in one of my favourite couplets from Blake:

> The Bat that flits at close of Eve
> Has left the brain that won't believe.

14th June, 2016

The sound of a lid on a nine-tenths-empty jar of honey being unscrewed and screwed back on again.

Last night, Bee-chan and I went to a book quiz evening at Blackwell's on High Holborn, where we made a team with Rudge.

Our team came fourth, I can't remember out of how many.

After the quiz itself, I was drawn particularly to the shelves where the Oxford University Press publications were on display. There were a handful of books that were of interest to me, but then a member of staff, apparently about to close the tills, asked if anyone still wanted to buy anything. I had already selected one book, but felt a little hurried in choosing a second—since, on those shelves, there was a two-for-the-price-of-one deal.

The first book I had selected was *The Natural History of Selborne*, by Gilbert White. The first lines on the back of the book were a quote from within:

> I was much entertained last summer with
> a tame bat, which would take flies out of
> a person's hand.

(Rudge seemed much amused when I pointed this quote out and told him this had sold the book to me.[1])

In a hurry, then, I chose my second book, which was *The Confusions of Young Törless*, by Robert Musil.

Later, on the train back to Barnehurst, Bee-chan took the Gilbert White book from me to have a look. She opened it at page 102, and there, immediately, my eye was caught by a quote from *As You Like It*:

> And tune his merry note
> Unto the wild bird's throat.[2]

I had plucked *As You Like It* from the shelves earlier, and might have bought that, rather than the Musil, had I not been so flustered. I have meant to read *As You Like It* for some time now, and specifically because I have long been fascinated with the song 'Under the Greenwood Tree', from which the above couplet was taken.

This, of course, is bibliomancy. It led me to *The Natural History of Selborne* and now leads me to *As You Like It*.

---

1 "They know how to sell a book," is what I actually said.
2 White misquotes Shakespeare. The original has "sweet bird's throat". Writing this footnote almost a year after the day in question—it is now the 13th of April, 2017—I remembered the page for the Shakespeare quote as 102. I looked there, and, not seeing it, spent much time leafing through the book again and again, start to finish, in order to find it. Eventually, I found it, where I had first looked, on page 102.

16th June, 2016

I am on the train from Waterloo to Reading and shall be disembarking at Richmond for the office. Ascot season is here, it seems. Men in top hats search for seats; all the women wear hats with webs of dotted gauze and orreries of feather on them, often aslant on their heads. A woman in a seat diagonally across from me is wearing a necklace so large and gaudy it looks like something an Aztec priest officiating at a human sacrifice might wear. English customs can sometimes seem deliberate and chunky, as English ceramics do, for instance, with their crude, cheerful floral patterns, when compared with Japanese ceramics, which, even among the affordable everyday pieces, have the appearance of subtle meditations on nature rendered in physical form.

It is true that I have often found English aesthetics superficial and uncouth. Perhaps by 'superficial' I mean 'lacking mystery'. At least there *is* an aesthetic that is recognisably English, however. I hope such cultural aesthetics endure. I would like us to be able to go on appreciating them, each by contrast with others, even when that contrast is unfavourable for this or that side. I don't want anyone to win.

*

It was past nine o'clock last night when I walked to the wood. When I emerged from the wood onto the park, I found that the meadow of lush grass I had walked in last time I was there had gone. I had plucked my specimens just in time. A mower had visited in the meantime and left no specimens to pluck. Lines of drying cut grass made furrows of the rolling turf, as if it were a ploughed field.

I used to love the smell of cut grass in summer. Perhaps I still do. I was deliberate enough to sniff for it on this occasion, and, sure enough, it was there, but seemed a dry, hay-like smell, lacking sweetness and piquancy. There was no hint of sehnsucht about it as there has been in former times.

I shouldn't exaggerate my feelings. The grass and weeds will grow again and I was not shocked. I had wondered how long the park could go unnoticed by civic authorities in its very tousled condition. It is a public space, and no doubt such long grass is inconvenient to people playing football and so forth.

Still, I had been looking at that grassy space closely enough recently to have some intimation of a whole world having disappeared. A miniature rainforest had been felled in one go. An invertebrates' megalopolis had been razed to the ground.

18th June, 2016

Yesterday, a minor event:

I took an earlier walk than usual in Bursted Wood. I was walking along the curving path which is perhaps the main artery of the wood, wider and more well-trodden than the others, and which has the carving of the snail at its edge, when I saw that one of my favourite trees was on fire. The base of this tree is very wide, but from this base grow six trunks, each as full and impressive as a mature, individual tree, and the place where these trunks meet forms a seat or basin in which I have stood on rainy days, or simply when no one is around. It was in this basin that someone had lit a fire. There were two people on the path ahead of me, a middle-aged man and a schoolboy. Neither paid the fire any attention. The schoolboy appeared curious at a distance, but, in fact, did not go near it.

My first confused impression, because there were people, was that the arsonists were present and I might have to confront them, but this proved not to be the case.

I approached and examined the fire. Some of the kindling was on the ground—magazines and school textbooks. The tree's basin was piled with smouldering and still flaming ashes. I was unsure what to do. There was no heavy rain. The fire might or might not go out of its own accord. I wondered how much damage was already done to the living tree. Four of the six separate trunks were scorched around the base.

Taking a stick from the side of the path, I fished some of the as yet unburnt material from the ashes, dropped it to the ground and stamped on it. I took one of the other magazines and used this to suffocate the flames on one of the magazines I'd just extracted from the fire. I poked at the ashes again but had the impression I was only stoking the fire up again by doing so. Therefore, I stopped. What else could I do?

I walked on but, by the time I'd arrived at the park, decided I should phone the fire brigade. I did not know the local number, so dialled 999.

After the call, I heard the siren in two or three minutes. I was beneath the trees again. I walked back to the park and saw a lone fireman. I hailed him and led him to the tree. With his radio he called for back up and "a couple of buckets of water".

Soon, three more firemen came, one wearing what he referred to as his "Ghostbusters pack". The buckets were poured on the fire, and the pack was used to finish the job off. The man who seemed in charge looked through the material that remained unburnt, some of which seemed to be an exercise book with a pupil's handwriting. They deduced that the arsonist was probably a girl, fifteen years of age. Mention was made of calling in "fire investigation".

A woman with her young son walked by. The boy said he'd never seen a real fire before and the firemen made the kind of remarks that fill young boys with admiration for them.

"I'm sure you're busy," I said at the end. "I wasn't sure whether to phone. I didn't want to waste your time."

"No, you did the right thing," said the one who had looked at the half-burnt books. "You never know, this could have spread." He looked up to the higher branches and laid his hand on one of the six trunks. "And damaged this tree."

"That's what I thought," I said.

There was a reason the book in Bee-chan's mother's living room was open at the pages concerning bats. It seems there had been bats in the garden and she had wanted to identify them. They were pipistrelles, she said.

Before she drove us into town, where some sort of street party had commenced, she also told us of something else she had observed in the garden in the last few days.

There had been a rat, and somehow it had caught a blackbird, which it was intent on carrying off, presumably for food. However, this was to prove no easy task, for it met with violent resistance. A number of other blackbirds, kin or kith of that in the rat's jaws, were dive-bombing the marauder. A lone blue tit had got in amongst them and had become a slightly incongruous ally in their manoeuvres. So spirited, in fact, was this defence of the fallen bird, that eventually the rat gave up its prey and scampered for the cover of the nearby bushes, hesitating and looking back before finally disappearing. Perhaps there were no winners here—I believe it was too late for the rat's victim. The other blackbirds, once the rat had gone, flapped to the ground and examined their fellow.

I thought about this story in silence during the car ride.

Public life demands words, but gardens do not, and this, perhaps, is one of the secrets of their appeal. If, to adapt the saying, an English person's home is his or her castle, then the garden is the courtyard, or, perhaps more tellingly, the cloister. I believe that, if we were to look for some physical representation of the spiritual life of England, we could do much worse than to settle on the garden. It is individual, personal, yet allows for the impersonal experience of nature. It is a place of letting-be and of contemplation without reference to denomination, and yet also without the tang of attitude that comes from equating rebellion with virtue.

The English are a formal and buttoned-up people, we are given to believe, and, among other things, their literature scorns metaphysics and concentrates on society. But much may be discovered between the lines, if we are attentive. The garden is a microcosm of the wild. Here, even with some relief, as we look from the kitchen window in simple, diurnal melancholy, we can confirm that there are events in the world other than the human, and they allow but do not require human commentary. The meaning of such events might be partially communicated, but they can be wholly understood only in silence.

22nd June, 2016

Listening to The Cure's 'Primary' recently, I find myself thinking that the atmosphere of this song, as of many other songs by The Cure, is made possible by a lack of explanation. The songs have an air of significance. To tie them either to atheism or to any faith that might be named, is to fold up meaning, emotion, atmosphere, like a fan.

Some trees have leaves around the bottoms of their trunks, making me think of the way that shire horses have white manes around their hooves.

This morning, from the window of the train from Bexleyheath to Waterloo East, I saw a young fox at the side of the track. Nothing very unusual in that, and yet its lively russet coat against the green of the grass was the colour of surprise and gladdened me.

The toilets at Waterloo East have been refurbished. It's about time. These were some of the worst public toilets I have ever had to enter in this country. Decline is not entirely universal, then.

At the Open Book today, I enquired after *The Blind Owl*. Apparently it's currently being reprinted. Having a little left on my book token, I looked around the shop. There was nothing that tempted me. I began to get that sensation common of late, that being more than halfway through my life now, I cannot afford to read omnivorously, but must be very selective. More than that, it is harder to luxuriate in the feeling that, as a reader, I am a coracle on an infinite sea of text. Soon, perhaps, I shall be cast up on some strange, final shore.

I was about the leave the shop, but glanced, cursorily, at the poetry section. The name 'John Clare' caught my eye. I picked up the book and read.

Some of the words within caught at some old corner of my heart.

Furze, ling and brake all mingling free.

An insect is addressed as a "tiney loiterer".

Somewhere there was a couplet that decided me, though I cannot now find which it was. I bought the book, using up the rest of my token and about three pounds more.

A while later I remembered why the name John Clare had particularly stuck in my mind. Peter Ackroyd had quoted him in *Albion*. He had grieved at the felling of a favourite tree, and written that he could not bear any longer to see the "inscapes" of the world destroyed. That stuck in my mind—trees are inscapes.

＊

I did not know which way to vote in the referendum. At first, I was thinking of voting Leave, but this was mainly instinct, backed by a few broad principles, and I have learnt that instinct can be prejudice or misapprehension, or at least needs careful training so that it can work with reason to examine a matter in depth.

Anyway, I did what research I could in the time I had, and in the end I voted Remain. On Facebook, just after I voted, I wrote, "The result of all I have read has been first to make me afraid of threats from one side, then from the other, and, finally, to slightly lessen my fears, in both directions. In any case, as far as I am concerned, the outcome of the vote and the fate of the country are now in the hands of God. *Homo proponit, sed Deus disponsit.*" The last, which perhaps I was too shy to write in English, being, "Man proposeth; God disposeth."

Then came the result, and I felt the shuddering shocks that others felt, as the ship of nation apparently struck a hidden rock. I was among those who desired— at least for a while and to an extent—a second referendum. But, after all, I refrained from signing the petition. Had I forgotten those words I had written? Was I afraid that God would dispose of the matter in the wrong way? But what, finally, does the saying mean? Is it advocating complete passivity? That cannot be true. A second referendum, after all, would merely be another proposition, for God to dispose of as it might.

So then, what *is* the meaning of the saying? Such sayings require meditation. They are not, I think, prescriptions for conduct, but means for settling the mind. You will do your best, but you cannot control everything. For the rest, you have a choice: to have faith or not. If you have faith there will perhaps be less gnashing of teeth in hatred, at least.

Five days later, while looking up Alcuin of York, I found this quote:

"*Nec audiendi qui solent dicere, vox populi, vox Dei, quum tumultuositas vulgi semper insaniae proxima sit.*"

That is:

"And do not listen to those who keep saying, 'The voice of the people is the voice of God', because the tumult of the crowd is always close to madness."

So, where do we hear the voice of God? How does God dispose of human proposals if not, again, through humankind? Well, there are events other than the human, of course, as I have noted. But there are many voices of the people; perhaps there are many voices of God, too. They are incoherent when you only hear the voices, but become coherent when you also hear the silence.

The shocks keep coming, and the situation seems only to have deteriorated since Friday, but strangely, today, as I write this, I am even beginning to think that my initial instincts were right and that when I reasoned myself to Remain, I had only reasoned myself halfway to the truth.

I do not know.

4ᵗʰ July, 2016

On Friday, the 1ˢᵗ, Bee-chan and I took a train from Paddington to Barnstaple, to attend A— and R—'s wedding on the 2ⁿᵈ.

We had used Air B&B in order to find somewhere to stay, in Bideford. It was an old building with art deco elements. The ground floor was a studio, filled with great earthenware heads. We were sleeping in a small mezzanine loft space. The first floor living room was also filled with clay heads and other bits and pieces. A simple cart—heavy planks on iron wheels—made a central table, emanating the peace of a rustic museum. I noticed the door to this space had the words "Board Room" on it, and the wood panelling around the walls repeated the art deco design visible on the building's façade.

On Saturday morning, Bee-chan went out for a run in the park. I went up to the kitchen in the hope of finding breakfast, but no one was around (see entry for the 6ᵗʰ of June). I supposed it would be okay to help myself, but was somehow hesitant. I decided to wait and, while I was doing so, looked a little around the living room.

There was a pile of large, hardback art books by an ottoman. On the spine of the second book from the top, the title *Damascus Tiles* caught my eye. I sat on the floor and began reading it.

Damascus Tiles, by Arthur Millner.

There are so many things in this world by which to be enchanted and fascinated, and there is, perhaps, only one short life in which to choose among them.

It was not John Clare who described trees as "inscapes",
it was Gerard Manley Hopkins, as I should have known.
However, Clare is mentioned in the same paragraph as
Hopkins in *Albion*, in the first chapter, 'Trees'.

I walked in Bursted Wood today at some time after
seven o'clock. I saw ash smeared on the trunk of one of
the trees. For some time now, the cow parsley has been
in a much reduced state. It has become skeletal, even
bent and broken. The stems are still largely green with
sap, though seeming to brown here and there, but the
flowers and leaves are gone. How swiftly the fullness of
growth passes.

The paths have dried up somewhat, returning
mainly to a pleasant dustiness, but there are still muddy
patches here and there, cratered with footprints. At a
bend in the path, the chiaroscuro on the ground captivated me—the play of light, gentle as it was soundless,
soothed me. It was the soft light of the evening sun
through the leaves, of course, stirred by breezes more
visible in this play than they were felt. Birdsong was the
perfect accompaniment.

I tried to think of the right word for the particular softness of this light, especially in combination with the dancing, spangled motion. The word that came to me was 'lambent', but this felt inadequate. It really can't be put into words, I thought, and this comforted me in some way. Then I thought perhaps it could, by a poet. Perhaps John Clare could put it into words. Perhaps even I could, with dedication and the favour of the right Muse.

I walked on. A young fox, ahead of me on the path, looked back over its shoulder, then disappeared.

In the park, I was drawn to the round-topped tree near one of the benches. I saw it was not as green and fresh even now, in early July, as it had been. Some of its twigs were bare, and some leaves were mottled with brown, as if burnt with too much sun. It looked a little rough and eaten away. Things in summer look like this sometimes—old and dusty and ragged at the edges.

Throughout the walk I was terribly distressed by the keen sadness of the passage of time. The movement of light and shadow—only this had soothed me.

There is a suggestion in this wonderful flickering that patterns repeat in a dance. Of course, this is precisely what Alan Watts says, for instance, in *Still the Mind*, which I re-read so recently. Nietzsche talked of eternal return, but was not the first to do so, I believe. Why should repetition be comforting or meaningful, some people ask. But perhaps it is more that the repetition is a way of explaining the meaningfulness of each moment. Which is not to say, either, that it is not literally true.

I took some leaves from the tree home with me, hoping to identify it, but it is proving strangely elusive. The leaves have three lobes each, and the tree also had wingnuts. I think it might be a kind of maple.

※

On Sunday, on the train between Barnstaple and Exeter—the Tarka Line—Bee-chan said early on, "Maybe we should split up."

A tear spilt down my cheek and I did not know what to say. Everything inside me seemed locked into a bitter fatalism.

It was a truly beautiful day—the kind of day for which I reserve the word 'halcyon', though perhaps I use that word incorrectly. The leaves seemed almost to dissolve in an ecstasy of sunlight. The train journey between Barnstaple and Exeter has long been one of my favourites, and I had long wanted to share it with Bee-chan on a day like this.

For a moment I thought how cruel it was that such a conversation would come at a time and place like this. The very beauty of the leaves and the sunlight seemed cruel.

When I was younger, it would have been at just such a moment that the imp of the perverse took charge of my heart. I would have thought, "So that's how it is!" I would have accepted the cruelty as my destiny, like a crown of thorns. I would have recklessly dragged everything down with me.

This time, I did not. I thought, after all, it was a beautiful day, and I did not want to waste this train journey with Bee-chan. A little further along, a slow bend in the river was framed in a break between trees. I pointed and Bee-chan looked, seemingly seeing just the beauty I saw.

I think, with this, the paralysis of bitterness ended, though not quite instantly. I have not asked her, but I wonder if Bee-chan felt this, too.

When we stopped at Eggesford Station, I took a photograph of her with the sun streaming through the train window and catching in her blue hair.

We clattered on towards Exeter. I remember the white flowers of convolvulus among the trackside luxuriance, peacefully sprawling. I remember a sign, "Cowley Bridge", flashing by, and the bridge itself, half-obscured by leaves, a mystery to my soul as inexplicably cool and refreshing as stepping into a river deep in a midsummer afternoon.

An example of the juxtapositions that regularly occur in my mind:

I had ordered a copy of *Strawberries* by The Damned for L—'s birthday and was listening to it again to reassure myself I'd made a good choice. I was reassured.

The album was released in 1982 and, indeed, I was taken back to that time. There was a particular kind of open-mindedness that I remember from that period that I struggle to find in the highly polarised social atmosphere of 2016. As I listened to the chugging guitars and blokey vocals, so real I could almost see the singer's nostril hairs, I had an image of a battered garden shed in which a scruffy but sensitive soul was discovering an unauthorised, DIY version of the meaning of life. The singing, far from autotuned, was not entirely melodic, but having the texture of life itself, finally, without triumph, as if haplessly, got behind the front line of my defences as a listener. I was not, in this relationship, the disciple or subject of an authority, but was also discovering, on an equal footing, the unauthorised meaning of life. Touches of whimsy in the melodies, piano trills and so on showed the liberating presence of the anima, not here needing to advertise itself in the manner of identity politics. The private experience of the singer and musicians was transmitted intimately to my private experience. We shared a garden shed.

A minute or two later, I saw a minor news item on Yahoo's news feed. It concerned little robot vehicles, like enlarged shoe brushes with wheels, that are now being introduced to replace the people on mopeds who deliver takeaway orders. The article was wholly positive in tone, talking of children hugging the lovable robots, and so on. I was utterly repulsed.

The world that was opening up in the garden shed in 1982 is closing down again, and fast, and seemingly with finality. There will be no garden shed for unauthorised discoveries anymore. The shed is fitted with CCTV. Whatever you do there is immediately the intellectual property of whoever owns the CCTV. They will disseminate it to a million automated mash-up content-feed sites before you can blink, so that there will be more instances of it being reproduced to computer sites and degraded by them, unread, unviewed, unembraced by understanding, than there are instances of being delivered to and known by a human being.

And yet, almost everyone I hear express an opinion seems to want more and more of this.

We are moving decisively away from, and not towards, any kind of world I want to live in. I am on the losing side, have already lost. The technophiles have won, and cheerfully accelerate their programme of making the world less and less human.

All the more reason for me to go my own way, since only my own lifetime, in the entire universe, will ever have any possibility of accommodating my way. The winners, who write history (if they still know how to write and still have the attention span for history) will forget me soon enough. How can they object, then, to my differing from them while I actually exist?

While I have been writing this entry I have been constantly interrupted by the loud, frequent auto-mated announcements at the train station and now in the train.

8th July, 2016

Of course, some might see the word 'human' as an insult, anyway. Conversely, the pejorative 'inhuman' suggests 'human' is an honourable title. On the whole—an appropriate phrase here—I prefer what I think is the common understanding of the word, denoting a flawed, vulnerable creature with an aspiring soul.

The transhumanist project, technological utopianism and so on, while apparently despising 'humanity', seem to me movements towards exaggerating and preserving in an indefinite loop all that is worst in humanity. The desire for control, for perfectionism, enshrines a repressed self-hatred that, in being repressed, is projected onto others. Transhumanists remind me always of that character in a film or story who abjectly and faithfully serves an evil master in the hope that he will be rewarded with a place of honour when that master's reign is established. It never works out that way in the stories, of course, and here I am inclined to believe the myth-making is true, but I suppose that I fear it is not.

So why is it that, particularly in relation to this subject matter, the faith I talk of in my entry for the 30th of June is uncertain?

✳

On Tuesday (the 5ᵗʰ) I had a conversation by Skype with Chris A. At some point he mentioned a quote he had encountered recently, though he could not recall the source. He quoted from memory and now I shall have to quote his quote from memory, so this will be inexact, but it was something like: "I know for a fact the soul exists and it is made one hundred per cent of attentiveness."

Sometimes a curious thought comes upon me when I am meditating. It is a question of sorts, and I don't know how to begin to answer it. I move my attention from the top of my head gradually to the tip of my toes. When it is at the top of my head, I feel the pleasant, uneven prickling of my scalp; when it is at my flank, I feel the tension of my skin, the weight of my flesh, and so on. And I wonder sometimes, what is attention? How does it move from one place to another? How do I move it?

Whatever attention is, there seems to be less and less of it in this age. My own attention span has been devastated by internet usage. Reading Karen Armstrong's *Fields of Blood* at the moment, I find I have to read almost every sentence two or three times. I notice these symptoms are worse when I have recently been exposed to the internet. Much of the internet is not even intended for a conscious audience. Soon, it seems, it will be produced wholly *by* bots *for* bots, and perhaps the light of self-awareness will go out on this planet, at least in the expanding 'developed' world.

Among my favourite authors are Mishima Yukio and William Burroughs, both of whom deal with a subject that I do not see much discussed, though it preoccupies me greatly. That subject is soul death. There is a hint of cosmic dualism about the idea of soul death, and I am not sure that I really believe in such dualism, and yet the idea of soul death haunts me terribly. Burroughs thinks the afterlife a possibility, but not guaranteed. He describes nuclear weaponry as something whose "secret function" is to be a "soul killer"—"to alleviate an escalating soul glut". I am not sure Mishima ever uses a phrase like "soul death" explicitly, but it is the central concern of *The Sea of Fertility*. The twentieth century has been deadly like no other, the underlying message seems to be, and the human soul has ebbed towards, and perhaps actually to, extinction.

A calculator and a human can both work out the sum 2+2, although perhaps it would be more accurate to say that the calculator does not work it out. It merely produces the answer, automatically. If it were faulty, it would not know. A human, producing the same answer, has also understood the answer, and the process by which it was attained. The Turing Test seems to imply that as long as the end result looks exactly the same, the one is identical to the other—all that is required is a very complex seeming. This is part of the current scientific project to eliminate the human soul. It is not truly, of course, a scientific endeavour—or not *prima facie*—but the current handmaidens of science—Daniel Dennett, Stephen Hawking, Lawrence Krauss and innumerable others—overwhelmingly seem to support it in one way or another. Ironically, in this respect, scientists are among the most powerful supporters of dumbing down, striving to eliminate consciousness itself.

Let us say there are three dimensions to consciousness, and, by tentative analogy, let us say that the vertical dimension is ineffable profundity (necessary to understanding, rather than mere efficient pattern-replication), the forward-backward dimension is functionality (all that is quantitative) and the left-right dimension is imagination; in this case, scientists are currently striving to eliminate the vertical dimension by which the other two dimensions might actually have any meaning.

It is attentiveness that increases the height and depth of this dimension. It is this that they wish to abolish. "Move along, nothing to see here," might be the motto of present-day scientists. Move along on the forward dimension, never stopping actually to see anything.

If this is read, it will be dismissed by many as an ignorant generalisation. I have noticed the tendency— others can judge where it is present and where absent, as I shall also continue to judge for myself.

I fear, anyway, that it is soul death that the transhumanists and their allies will achieve. Whatever he might have been wrong about, Marx was correct in diagnosing alienation as the primary problem of human history. Locked into a self-worship indistinguishable from self-hatred, the transhumanists will not replace humanity with liberation, but with the very quintessence of alienation—the anti-soul, humanity banished forever. It would be better to rot in the soil and become one with what is other than human. The transhumanist aspiration is an old one in a new form; they aspire to be undead.

Quite a satisfying walk earlier today.

On reflection, I decided that this was at least partly because I had taken my camera. Before I went out, I'd been watching some ridiculous talk show thing about the end of the world. The one really intelligent point I saw made as I skimmed through it, was by a woman from the *Guardian*, who said that, of course, the planet would survive because we would destroy ourselves before we could destroy the planet. This is obvious and not original, but it is also true and is often forgotten and she expressed it well. Funnily enough, the effect of this programme was momentarily to put me in a mood that, it occurred to me, was akin to what is sometimes called 'grace'. I once formulated this idea or feeling in the following question, which I now remembered: "What if the world was exactly as it is now but good?"

So, I stepped out in a good mood. It was soon diluted with other thoughts and feelings, but not too badly.

When I came to Bursted Wood, I saw the lambency previously mentioned on the path again. I decided to try and record it, using my camera's film function for the first time (not deterred by my usual technophobia).

I made two such films. It was interesting playing them back, seeing the shadows in them move differently to the shadows moving on the ground at the moment I was replaying them. It really was as if the camera held a little rock pool of time, different to the tide of time around it, though originally from that tide.

A sunny, peaceful day in the middle of July. I plucked a couple of white convolvulus flowers, and put them in my pocket for the vase at home. I remembered that convolvulus had been my favourite flower when I was a youth. I thought, after all, it might still be.

I took various photographs in the course of my walk.

As I was on my way back home, it occurred to me that the photographs had contributed to my sense of well-being. We hear a lot about the recording of moments, with cameras and so on, taking you out of the moment, but, after all, perhaps this is not always so—perhaps the opposite is sometimes true. Even, more often. If I think of my experience of photography, it seems to be. And I am glad if photography can help us appreciate the moment, because I would like this to extend to the arts generally—the attempt to freeze things in time.

From John Clare's 'The Moorhen's Nest':

> And then I walk and swing my stick for joy
> And catch at little pictures passing by:
> A gate whose posts are two old dotterel trees,
> A close with molehills sprinkled o'er its leas.

We instinctively try to capture the moment. A photograph is a way of reminding us that a moment, indeed, can be framed for appreciation. We become conscious of our mental framing when we have a more literal form, and so we can appreciate the less literal form all the more. Ultimately, it is the mental framing that is primary, though the literal form has its advantages. Those advantages are nothing if they do not serve the primary framing, the essential framing, of our mind.

12th July, 2016

An ordinary life. By what standard? For a moment I felt like a hang glider, in a rapid but descending flight above treetops, my legs dangling, knowing that I might injure them, but thinking that, after all, it is quite possible that I will land safely, and in the meantime, there is nothing to which the sensation might be compared.

15th July, 2016

On Tuesday, after seeing *Il trovatore*, Bee-chan and I took the train from Charing X to Bexley, whence we caught a bus to Bexleyheath.

Near us, in one of the seats by the door between our carriage and the next, a middle-aged man with something of a paunch had been chatting to some women. They were about to get off the train and the man expressed his fear that he would now have no one to wake him when it came to his station (which was Crayford, I believe).

"We're getting off at Bexley," Bee-chan volunteered. This was the stop before Crayford, so not too bad as a place to have a wake-up call.

"See," said the man, "we all love each other really."

Being something of a phlegmatic creature, I sometimes have to force an outward show of reaction for the sake of politeness. That is, I think, there is usually a disconnect between my inner workings and my outward demeanour. In order to express the inner approval I felt at this sentiment, and not knowing quite what to say, I forced myself to smile. To my horror, as I did so, I also seemed to be inadvertently forcing a scoffing, snorting noise in my throat and nose, as of derision. In fact, I think this was not mechanical, but a real, organic response arising from some obscure—almost atavistically obscure—embarrassment.

"We do! We do!" protested the man.

Although, strangely, I think he began his protest a microsecond before my snort. It was hard to tell.

What I really felt in response to his words was affirmation and a kind of pathos. It was that word— "really". In other words, despite overwhelming appearances. They were words spoken in the face of sadness. I wondered what had been the particular sadness that had prompted the man. I remember the quote: "Everyone you meet is engaged in a great battle. Be kind."[1] I could think of various sources of sadness that made me respond to his words, some of them more personal than others. In some sense on the less personal level, for instance, there has been all the tremendous division and enmity that has arisen in the wake of the Brexit vote. I also thought of the opera we had just seen, in which two brothers, separated in early life, become rivals and enemies. The central truth of the story is that they are brothers—thus their enmity is a tragedy. That they are brothers is the secret that must be remembered, corre-

---

1 This quotation tends to be attributed to the Revered John Watson, also known as Ian Maclaren. I have reproduced it here in the form that I believe I first encountered it. Searching online now, I find forms that put the injunction to "be kind" at the beginning of the quote predominate. I prefer the version I have used here, which to me is primary, since the construction is more suggestive: First comes the state of affairs, then the injunction that logically follows from and yet sits in opposition to that state.

sponding to the man's "really". There were other, more personal things on my mind, too.

So, I felt as if the man had unconsciously taken part in a conversation in my own heart. He had spoken in that timely way that feels like a message addressed to us by the world. After all, I don't find this fanciful.

Sadly, I had responded with hesitation and embarrassment, unsure how to make the truth I felt inside sound convincing when conveyed to the outside world, because of this miserable disconnect of outer and inner from which I have suffered for the greater part of my life.

I often express love through duty. Or, I feel easier using the second word, acting according to it. So, although the man was still wide awake when we got to Bexley, I said, "Crayford is the next stop" as we were getting off. But the man was intent on his smartphone, texting, I think, and seemed not to hear.

As we walked away from Bexley Station, I tried to explain to Bee-chan that I felt bad about my response to the man, but I don't think I was able to communicate my feelings clearly.

"Anyway, why did he say that to you when it was me who offered to wake him?" said Bee-chan.

"Exactly," I said, though I have no idea what I meant by this, unless it was simply a way of validating my confused reaction to him.

16th July, 2016

A muggy day. Earlier, the air smelt gummy, as if particles of dust had been steamed off the pavements to mix with sticky pollen. This kind of day reminds me a little of Japan. It's just after six thirty p.m. and I'm on my way to Dominika's party. There are clouds low in the sky, their bellies a dark grey, but no rain has fallen as yet.

On Sunday the 10th I went for a walk, as described. While walking along the main path of Bursted Wood I saw a family coming the other way. As I recall, there were two young boys haring ahead of a man and a rather large, tattooed woman. The woman shouted at the boys to "ask the man", meaning me, of course. They didn't listen to her, so when she was closer she asked me herself where the wooden snail was—it was just along the path.

"It's Pokémon, you see," she said. "Gotta get 'em all."

I did not understand this remark at the time. I thought she meant that the boys were intent on seeing all the carvings as one might collect Pokémon cards.

The next day, on the internet, I read an article about the—newly released, it seems—Pokémon Go. The article claimed that the game was a force for good, citing the author's own experience of how, while playing it, he had been hailed by some "sketchy" black dudes who had told him where to find whatever it was the game required (which I don't remember), and had ended up chatting with them and, when a policeman had come over to see what was going on, explaining to the policeman about Pokémon Go and converting him on the spot.

This did, indeed, seem a positive story. I questioned my usual reservations without arriving at any definite conclusions. I only thought it was a shame people needed an excuse to go for a walk and chat to strangers, and also felt a vague sense of violation that Bursted Wood had been used as part of the Pokémon project. What was that project, exactly? Whatever it was, I was irritated by the impression they had electronically marked their territory in the wood. I doubted they had any actual interest in the wood for its own sake, and the boys I had seen, after all, had not really been interested in the wooden carvings. They might become interested by association, of course.

The next day again, I saw another article about Pokémon Go. I could not quite work out its tone. Was it sarcastic or sincere? It suggested, anyway, that the game was part of a military surveillance operation.

The terms and conditions as quoted in the article appear real enough, granting Pokémon Go greater powers even than Google currently ask for:

> We may disclose any information about you (or your authorized child) that is in our possession to government or law enforcement officials or private parties . . .

I have always been in favour of a lifelong valuing of childhood, but there is something strange about the current fixation with childish things that is apparent in the (so-called) first world. Or is this simply the natural result of the values I have long held, finally triumphing? Is it, so to speak, a case of 'be careful what you wish for'? What I feel, anyway, is, "I didn't mean it like this."

17ᵗʰ July, 2016

Quite a hot day and I am on the train from Bexley to Waterloo East. I hoovered and mopped the floor earlier, and sweat began to drip from my brow.

I noticed the vending machine at Bexley Station was less than half stocked. There is a pathos, sometimes, about vending machines. They speak of the activity of absent humans. I imagine the sadness of putting coins into one after some kind of apocalypse.

Last night, at the party, one of Dominika's friends, hearing that I'm a writer, asked me immediately whether I wrote about the inner journeys of my characters. I hemmed and hawed a little but conceded that there was a lot of interiority to what I wrote. Again immediately, she asked whether there was any readership for that anymore given the death of the author, etc. "There is no more interior," she said. Or, actually, "The interior is dead." I know, anyway, the pronouncement-of-death meme was used at some point. I particularly dislike that meme, as I tend to believe it's more a kind of wishful thinking than anything else, and so I felt somewhat defensive. "Everything is surface now," she said. I felt she was implying that because "everything *is* surface" everything *should be* surface—a common blurring of is and ought, and particularly common in enforcing the authority of cultural trends.

However, I decided not to be hasty and in the end I was not sure she was actually advocating this. She seemed simply to be asking questions. Unfortunately, I have been made sensitive to these particular questions, and winced inwardly as if probed in a sore place by a medical examiner.

Anyway, she was entirely right that the tendency is towards a celebration of the surface and a disdain of interiority. I was reminded, talking with her, that this is the orthodoxy in the arts now, too, so that the human soul faces a double-pronged attack from the battalions of resentment in both science and so-called humanities. The Turing Test is all about surfaces, too. The point is merely to appear a certain way. All cultural forces are now complicit in this.

She was also right—this is a commonplace, but true—in identifying this worship of surface with the decline of religion. Or at least, she was right in the following sense. There is no necessary reason why a decline in religion should lead to a rise in superficiality, depending on one's definition of 'religion'. I would say that 'sacred values' are possible without religion. In fact, I would say the former are essential to human life; I am not yet convinced this is true of the latter. However, the modern, deliberate emphasis on superficiality is basically a malicious and perpetual attempt to be revenged upon the perceived historical enemy, religion. The humanists, associating depth, interiority and so on with religion, intending to finish religion off, tighten their grip as they strangle the human soul.

I noticed, however, that later on she used the word 'soul' in a positive sense. If I recall correctly, saying that artists and writers need to choose pseudonyms that resonate with their work and their soul.

Another hot day. I have windows open in the kitchen, bathroom and bedroom. I cleared the floor to hoover and mop yesterday, with the result that the sofa is piled with books. The task now is to put things away so as to maximise space and minimise clutter. In the meantime, the sunlight on the wider-looking expanse of the cleared and cleaned sitting room floor gives a serene impression.

Even in a suburb like this, in the 21st century, noise is never-ending—traffic noise, mainly. The worst are the helicopters that mysteriously circle the southeast of London. They seem forever about to depart and then maddeningly circle back in a loop whose position you can never quite place. I have often wondered whether it is possible to listen to such noises without at least some disturbance of emotion. Today, something in the quality of the sunlight seems to bring me closer to that possibility. I think I even achieved it for a few minutes.

I sat down on the gleaming floor to meditate and picked up my round, white teacup, in which was the yellow-amber, half-roasted genmaicha. I blew on it, and shadows of the ripples played on the bottom and curved sides of the cup. Then I set the cup down and closed my eyes. From somewhere there came a noise like roadworks—a percussive chugging—and a clanging as of a metal scaffold pole being dropped on concrete. But these sounds were softened, even silky, as if the hot sun itself had melted their rough edges, dissolving them into a caress.

Some minutes later, the overlapping, relentless approach and departure of car engines began to annoy me again. When will their business ever be finished?

19ᵗʰ July, 2016

On train from New Cross—the Ginger Line. A chap on the train unrolled a prayer mat and, with his shoes to one side, was bowing, presumably in the direction of Mecca. I'm not sure I've ever seen that before—certainly not on a train.

On Sunday, at John C.'s birthday party, his friend John remarked disparagingly that the paper he'd been reading—he brandished the offending rag, *The Observer*, if I recall correctly—had reported that a cure has now been found for Dutch elm disease and that, therefore, our country's Dutch elms will now be saved. "It is the disease, not the elms, that is Dutch," he fulminated, highly indignant at said paper's pro-European ignorance.

I had not heard mention of Dutch elm disease in an exceedingly long time. Its mention now triggered a peculiar kind of nostalgia in me. There was an image and a feeling buried in some deep stratum of my memory, where memory begins to turn into soul, that related to the words 'Dutch elm disease'.

After the party, John's mention of the newspaper article came back to me and I contemplated that image and that feeling quietly, at leisure.

We had been told about Dutch elm disease when I was at primary school, back in Combe Martin. It is perhaps the earliest memory I retain of knowledge of a creeping doom at work in the world around me, rather than before I was born or in a story. No doubt I encountered all kinds of reports from which I might deduce the impermanence of all I loved, but Dutch elm disease remained distinct in my mind. It stands out even now from the mist of the past. The trees withered, eaten away inside, and there was nothing that could be done to stop it. The process was slow, but inexorable, and although the future was shrouded in ultimate uncertainty, if nothing changed, a day would come, in my lifetime, when there were no more elm trees in England, which was to me, at that age, virtually the world.

It was not merely a feeling of sadness that this gave me. There was something sinister in the blight—it was an unfeeling encroachment upon all that was familiar and good.

And the image I retain is of a single tree, in one of the fields where I used to play, "down Crackalans", as we used to say. The tree was afflicted with the malaise in question, its trunk becoming a husk, its branches snapped and jagged. It simply stood there in the field, surrounded by a field's usual silence, a picture of the doom I feared, accomplished. There will be more like this, it seemed to say. This is the end awaiting all things.

And there was nothing that could be done. And it was quiet, quiet, horrible and ultimate in a peaceful nightmare.

I remembered and considered all this. And now they have a cure? Well, that's a relief, I thought. But it was not a great relief, because I had ceased to worry about the elms long ago, and now had transferred my worry to other things.

It suddenly occurred to me, though—I'd like to be able to go back and tell the boy I was, "They find a cure. Don't worry."

Earlier today the moon seemed huge, bloated, and tinged with yellow and orange. I saw it again, at around midnight, and in the full dark it had turned silver once more, and shrunk to its normal size . . . over the rooftops of Shrubland Road.

20th July, 2016

There's something I've been meaning to write about here for a while. Looking back over the pages of my daily diary, I see that it took place on the 4th of June.

Bee-chan and I had been invited for dinner near Turnpike Lane. Afterwards, we made our way to a bus stop (to take the number 67, if I remember correctly). In the bus shelter was one of those video posters that are becoming prevalent, making it harder and harder to escape the kind of adverts that were once only shown during television breaks. The video in this case— looped, as these things always are, of course—showed a girl of perhaps thirteen stepping through the door of her home, apparently having just returned from school. She was alone and there was no one to welcome her. Instead, she looked warily to left and right, almost as if she were afraid someone might be there who shouldn't. Below this video image were a number of messages of the digital update variety. Next to the time signature for each were simple bulletins, such as, "Michael—seen." The girl, Lisa, let's say, was now also "seen", as the home security camera focused on her features and matched them to the facial features in the system's memory. This information was then relayed to the absent parents who could thus keep close surveillance on their home and their children's movements.

My mood sank considerably when I saw this advert. In fact, it seemed both of us found it creepy.

When we got on the bus, Bee-chan asked me what was wrong with having a security system of that kind. I must have spluttered or raised my voice when I replied, because she protested that she didn't like it either, but she didn't know why. Was it an irrational aversion?

I realised the advert really had set me on edge. I calmed myself and tried to answer her question. As I recall now, I divided what I thought was wrong with this kind of surveillance into three broad categories, as follows:

1. *Where will it end?* I thought this was the easiest category to grasp. We are using this technology now simply because we can and because we are very desirous of safety and maintaining control of our environment. This security system *could* save your daughter from an axe murderer (to name one unlikely scenario). How would you feel knowing you had refused to install such a system if she really were murdered? And so these systems have an inexorable logic of proliferation. They are not only understandable, it becomes 'backwards' to refuse them. But the technology will develop further and further, and there will always be some bad thing that *can* and then *must* be prevented that justifies us using every

technology that is made. What, then, when we can read people's very thoughts? Will we make thought crime a literal reality? I assume in this scenario there will be asymmetrical power. Those higher up in society will have filters not available to those lower down, which will screen their thoughts.

2. *The value of solitude.* As these systems become general, we might see (literally see) a whole generation growing up who never know what it is like not to be watched. Psychologically, they will always be self-conscious, performing for hidden or visible cameras. Even before their thoughts can be read, the sense of never being alone will strangle the knowledge that they are free in their own minds. Such freedom of thought is vital to the workings of conscience and of creativity. There is also a dimension to the value of solitude that is necessarily hard or impossible to express. "Uncontradicting solitude," Larkin called it. What could be more essential to spiritual health? And this, of course, also highlights the distinction between solitude and loneliness. These future generations might never know solitude, but it is easy to imagine they will be immersed in a greater loneliness than ever before—the loneliness of seeing and being seen, but being unable to speak and afraid even to think.

3. *The value of the wild.* When all that is important is to control one's environment, what happens is that the wild is abolished. Nothing outside the

box of knowledge and control must be allowed. That box becomes the world. Control breeds incestuously with control, so that human experience is a form of recursive and ever-shrinking tunnel vision. At some point, in fact, this must mean the abolition of humanity itself.

When I get to number three, when the light at the end of the tunnel-vision seems to shrink to nothingness and utter darkness, hope begins to stir in me again. Is it even possible to control the environment to this extent? Sooner or later, all that is repressed in one place must erupt violently elsewhere. And even supposing humans manage to control their own environment completely—thereby ceasing to be living beings—even supposing such a thing is logically possible, let alone practically possible, does it not, after all, simply amount to a divorce? The wild will continue to exist elsewhere in some form—it is only that humans will no longer know anything of it.

Our current obsession with surveillance is another kind of arms race. It escalates and escalates, because the logic of our society makes it inevitable, but the ultimate conclusion of that logic is slavery, destruction, or both.

But the hope that arises in me when the dot of light is about to vanish made me question why my intuition so strongly alerts me to evil in the presence of this escalation. I am, at least to an extent, a horror writer. As Michel Houellebecq has observed, we are professionally aware of evil. Perhaps I am simply more than commonly sensitive, or perhaps I am inclined to exaggeration in this area.

What is evil? I asked myself, by no means for the first time. The difficulty is, it so often poses as good. The advertised surveillance was driven by what we might call 'family values'. Perhaps that is a clue, but it is not the ultimate answer.

I was, by this time of the night, a little hazy with alcohol, but suddenly something occurred to me as if it were, indeed, the answer to the question. If you take the yin-yang symbol and remove the dots, you have a diagram of evil. We need those dots of mutuality. Evil is not on one side or another, but shifts and swirls. Only the understanding represented in those two dots can do anything to weaken its powers.

This, of course, is not an original insight, and I do not know how deep it takes us into the human dilemma, but it seemed to me, at the time, worth remembering.

21ˢᵗ July, 2016

Beautiful monstrous buddleia bush looming over someone's garage.

Unless I scrawl on the unlined brown flypaper at the end (which I might), I have less than two pages till I fill this notebook, and I told myself from the start I would fill this notebook and let that decide the end of this particular piece of writing. Now that I am so close to finishing, I feel quite sad. This is unusual. I do not usually feel sad when I finish written work. Why this time? Precisely because of time, I think, because I have been measuring and examining it and it has passed. It is also true that there are many more things I would have liked to include here—notes on changes in rainfall over the years, the winter twittering of birds that was an early herald of spring, a reminiscence on visiting a friend (do I still have space?), and so on. I'll allow myself one addition to the length of this notebook. Should this be published, which is my intention, I shall append the dream I had of Geoffrey of Monmouth, which does not seem inappropriate.

I suppose the cure for Dutch elm disease should incline me to view science more favourably, but despite my on-going efforts I find it nigh on impossible to see science as ultimately benevolent, or even neutral. Yes, I am more or less persuaded that the laws of thermodynamics are beautiful, as I am told, but what does that matter when we are destroying the visible beauty around us along with our very ability to appreciate beauty in the form of human consciousness? There are scientists who wish to rouse us to some kind of action to mitigate the worst effects of climate change, but apart from their abysmal performance in spreading the information itself, how can they expect to motivate us when the only future their science offers us is one in which humanity is, anyway, abolished? Hawking and others have banded together to warn us that Artificial Intelligence could be the equivalent of an alien invasion, but I see no evidence of soul-searching in the scientific community regarding the various demons science has unleashed, and continues to unleash. They seem to consider they have a manifest destiny.

I am told—and will be again—that science is merely a method and is distinct from what we do with the method. In short, science is not technology. Yet when-ever I express doubts as to the positive influence of sci-ence in our lives, I am inevitably opposed by someone who points to technology (usually meaning electronics and so on) as the very thing that indicates the inarguable goodness of science.

Earlier this week, Facebook threw up a 'suggested post' that was a Buzzfeed article listing eleven things that will no longer exist in ten years' time. The list—written in that dumbed-down 'science says' kind of way that I'm sure is a deliberate tactic to get past people's defences—included such things as 'drivers', 'delivery people' and so on. It ended with 'offline'. The 'internet of things', it told us, will mean there will never be a moment we are not connected to the web.

I saw that the post was sponsored by the tech site Cisco. So, essentially they are using one of the trashiest sites on the internet to pump out their propaganda.

It occurs to me that technophiles will, if this situation transpires, render one of their constant retorts obsolete. I have been told numerous times on the internet that the fact I am communicating via the internet deprives me of any right to complain about science. In the near future envisioned, if such a person sneers in the habitual way of their kind, "You're using the internet. You can't complain about science if you're using the internet," I shall, sadly with no sense of triumph, reply, "Offline has been abolished, as you know. I'm afraid that neither of us are using the internet. It is using us."

1st August, 2016

Written in anticipation of October:

> What can we say of
> Past favourites, warm as grey clouds?
> It used to be my
> Favourite month, favourite novel,
> Favourite song—I remember.

What would make me happy? To sit at a desk in a warm, quiet room, to look out the window at a cloudy sky, and to write. Simply to be able to do this without stress or distractions, until I die. I no longer require the adventures that in youth I wished to measure and prove myself against. Even the emptiest day brings me more than enough matter to deal with.[1]

---

1 The notebook ends here, but, contrary to my original intentions, I recorded a little more of the year in a separate notebook.

2nd August, 2016—Aachen

To be afraid of death is to distrust the universe. Why would you want to stay alive in a universe you distrust?

10th August, 2016

So, it is a Tuesday. You are met at the train station and shown to the apartment where you will be spending a single night. You are filled with the deep exhaustion of early rising and travel over long distances—an exhaustion that does not centre in particular areas of the body but seems to permeate body and mind evenly, almost with a kind of sweetness. It is like feeling air stirring in a great cavern. The friend of the apartment's owner hands the keys over to you. He has no wish to linger and soon leaves you to the empty freedom of your vacation.

It is raining from smeary grey skies as you head out towards St. Mary's Cathedral where some relics of Charlemagne are kept in a casket. The cathedral will close soon. There is just time to look around a little, at the mosaics on the walls and ceiling, and the soaring stained-glass windows, which are of a much more recent date than the cathedral itself. This town was once a centre for culture in Europe.

Bee-chan lights a candle.

Out you go, again, into the old, rainy streets. You don't know what to eat, but settle on a touristy Italian

181

place, sitting outside, under the awning, though the weather is still dismal. You drink a glass of Vermentino and decide it is good, as if you know about such things.

You are both still tired, however, and return to your apartment. The bedroom window shows an unremarkable view of the roofs and walls of houses, of greenery here and there, of clouds and rain. It is not impressive, but beauty hides within it as rain hides in the cloud.

The wind of tiredness blows through you, driving the images of the day through your mind like clouds through the sky. You lie down upon the bed, the images still driven upon that wind, in waking or in sleep—it is the same. The sweetness of that exhaustion. Since you know that death, of necessity, must be trusted, you can surrender. If that sweetness were to carry you on its wind out of this world entirely, it would be no cause for regret. It has been a perfect day, perfectly inconsequential.

I think it was on the 5th of August, in Wacken, that, with rain falling on the tent and our muddy, booted feet protruding from the flap into the outer air, I read to Bee-chan Werther's letter of the 21st of June, 1771.

On Saturday, the 6th, in the morning, a dark cloud hung a spiked devil's tail over the camp site. Lightning

182

flashed, then came thunder and the rain began to beat down heavily. Once more we sheltered in the tent, this time feeling it shudder with the strength of the wind.

When the storm had passed, we emerged. Sunlight was creeping back like a second dawn. Swallows flew here and there just above the height of the tent poles, like pennants of peace; some nameless victory had been secured and, if only we knew how to recognise it, some nameless gladness was to come.

It was the Thursday or the Friday at Wacken—I think, the Thursday, that is, the 4th of August. Dan and I were in that part of the festival grounds that had been contrived to look somewhat like a mediaeval village. It is true that the resemblance had only a theme-park level of accuracy, but even this much was pleasing, perhaps because a great deal of wooden structure was involved. There were stalls selling drinking horns and others selling mead-beer and smoke from different sources drifted pleasingly on the air. In one part of this 'village', two whole pigs were revolving on spits. Their legs were drawn up as if they had been slain at some moment of the activity that characterised their life, perhaps the very activity of trying to escape death.

Darkness was just falling. We were waiting for Beechan and a little at a loss as to how to pass the time. Dan had anxious concerns about what awaited him on our return to England. I was not much looking forward to the return either. I suggested we go over and watch the blacksmiths. "Fire is always good," I said. "You can't get bored of watching fire." Dan seemed to concur. Certainly there was comfort to the orange glow of flames in the gloom.

I began to think of *The Sorrows of Young Werther*, which I had been reading. "Something that has occurred to me as I've been reading," I said, "is to do with what might have been lost since those times. Of course, we have no way of really knowing without travelling in time whether life was better or worse then than it is now, but *Werther* gives me an idea that it's possible some things were better. People always talk about the increase of technology and how it's eliminated many of the hardships of life, and because this is quite concrete, it's hard to argue against. But what we might have lost, though it is less concrete, might be just as important as what we've gained, or even more important.

"There's a sense in *Werther* that people interacted more directly, more elementally with their environment then than they do now—it was possible to have a more profound experience of your own existence as part of the world. For instance, there's a scene where he goes to a spot by the river where people gather water and it's something like a sacred place. And something like this—working as a blacksmith—working directly with fire and iron and being in charge of the making of something, doesn't leave much room for the kind of alienation described by Marx."

"Yes," responded Dan, "it's something to do with the opportunity for apperception. It's something of a cliché, of course, but it's like the Zen idea of trying to get the perfect brushstroke or the perfect stroke of an axe. In paying close attention to your environment and to a particular task and the tools and materials you're working with, your awareness itself expands and becomes more finely attuned."

And we talked again about Zoroastrianism and Heraclitus. Eternal fire—I now saw something truly profound and consoling, even compassionate, in the idea. Ever-changing, it is, nonetheless, ever the same, undying soul. What light and shadows did these flames make on our faces? Even to see a happy time pass can bring a sadness like grief—even, that is, passing from one happy time to another. When you are crowded about by worries, the grief is keener yet, and has a more resounding ache. All of us must die, and before we do love is shipwrecked, there are partings, dreams are seen to fail, bad rumours circle like scavenging wolves. Still, this fire never dies. Always somewhere in the dark, this same dance of warmth and light.

Though time was and is passing for us, too, to stand talking by the fire was not a waste of it, and the memory is a strange and indescribable consolation to me.

According to my calendar, we enter autumn later this month. This will be the last entry I write in this diary. I am writing in a mood of great uncertainty regarding my own personal future and that also of the human species.

Recently there was a message thread on TLO that started with a link to something on Drap's blog—an entry in which he quoted Ligotti as saying he was "a liberal who desires the extinction of the human race". Drap expressed the view that this remark summed up the 'progressive' tendency, that it was towards this that modern progress was heading.

I also distrust modernity and also see it tending in the same direction, but I am not sure that I blame liberalism as such for this (besides which, the word has so many meanings, under at least one of which, I probably am liberal). There are many modern attitudes of which I am suspicious, but I can usually find some good in them, some justification for their existence. It seems to me there is one underlying thing that always swings the balance in favour of hatefulness and destruction, and that is materialism. And that from which materialism derives its supposed authority? The answer is science.[1] Of course, science is only intrinsically materialistic in the sense it has no authority beyond matters of matter, but in the lust for greater authority, and perhaps more especially, greater power, there are many, it seems, who try to force upon us the view that nothing exists outside the jurisdiction of science—outside matter. The result is that science no longer serves humanity but is inimical to humanity. I greatly fear that Lovecraft was correct when he wrote that science would be "the ultimate exterminator of our species".

When I think of what the transhumanists propose to do, it seems to me that with their rise, the outcome of all evolution and history will be the triumph of evil. And following this train of thought, overcome by despair, I ask myself, can the universe be anything other than evil in which such a triumph takes place?

I have to remind myself that there are good reasons not to be a Manichean.

I have noticed, from time to time, an antidote to this despair within me. I simply remember the people in my own life, the feeling of their presence, their voices, their day-to-day concerns. This is what the transhumanists wish to abolish—humanity. But here it is. Here it is, flowering in the hedgerow of the universe itself. It comes from the universe. Where will it go? It

---

1 I am often told by a friend mentioned in these pages that for the meaning I intend in this case I should use "the natural sciences"; we should remember that 'science' once meant, and should still mean, something much larger.

is here. Where will it go? It is here. Where will it go? It is here.

It is a very ordinary thing to do, to live in the moment. Then we are told the wise person thinks of the future. The transhumanist wants to own the future, and by seizing it, to transform the present, abolish the past. The sage tells us once more to live in the moment. Isn't that what we were doing in the first place, as the ordinary human fools we are?

Perhaps there is no future for the transhumanists to seize.

In 1955, when Michele Besso died, Einstein wrote to his family: "Now he has departed from this strange world a little ahead of me. That means nothing. People like us, who believe in physics, know that the distinction between past, present and future is only a stubbornly persistent illusion."

A message from an age when scientists still had some grasp of the philosophy from which they are descended, and a shred of humanity.

I write this on a chilly evening after many days of heat. The fridge has just started its cricket-song. Somewhere in the distance I hear drunken voices.

Why do we continue to have children?

Appendix:
Geoffrey of Monmouth (a Dream)

In fact, I had this dream sometime during the night of the 31st of January/1st of February. I believe the dream itself was long and complex, but I have salvaged from it a single image-fragment with its attendant mental background. I woke up with the need to look up Geoffrey of Monmouth on the internet.

The fragment of dream is merely this. Somewhere in a large building were extensive bookshelves. A finger—probably mine—was placed at the top of the spine of one of the books on one of these shelves. It was a thick, ancient book, tooled and embossed and of a large format, as some of the older kinds of encyclopaedia were, or the sets of classics. In fact, this book was the first of a many-volumed set, the other volumes of which sat on the same shelf.

The finger pulled out the book and next I saw the finger following the words of the first line of the first page. If I was able to read actual words in the dream, I cannot now remember them. I know, however, that this set of books was Geoffrey of Monmouth, though now I am not sure whether that meant the title of the work, the author, or whether it somehow indicated the books were a kind of gestalt entity called Geoffrey of Monmouth. Perhaps there was not a clear distinction between these categories in the dream and the designation indicated all three meanings.

As I read, slowly, from this ponderous work, it seemed that I was questioned. I am not sure who questioned me, or in what words, but the spirit of their question was to express doubt that a work such as this could be of any interest. Here, 'interest' expresses both relevance to life today and excitement. The same voice seemed to suggest to me that, in the old days when this book was written, writers would have had very little competition for the attention of the reader, and therefore, their ideas of what would form a stimulating narrative would have been extremely limited and naïve; in short, the book was utterly obsolete. Not only that, the same lack of competition meant that they could extend their very plain fare over volume after volume after volume. To read it would be intolerable. It might take a lifetime and offer only so much benefit in information and entertainment as might be found in a few paragraphs of a modern short story.

Did I really propose to read this entire set of books, the voice asked.

What the voice had said had, indeed, greatly shaken my confidence. It seemed to me that it could be true— was even probable—that the entire work was obsolete. Yet this was what I had chosen to read in preference to any other written work. I had started it—though only just—and I intended to finish it. I even had an obscure faith in it, though—since I had not yet read it—I did not know why. I was committed to it now, and accepted that my fate was to read it, whether it was a waste of time or not.

Even while I was still asleep, I repeated to myself, over and over, the name 'Geoffrey of Monmouth'. I was, to some degree, lucid-dreaming, since my intention was to remind myself to look up the name when I awoke (which I did). I believe I first encountered the name in *The Oxford Illustrated History of English Literature*, which I was reading some time around 2007 or 2008. I do not recall ever being conscious of the name since then, and it is a little odd to me that my unconscious mind should insist on the name with such emphasis eight years after I last was conscious of it.

Looking the name up on the 1st of February, I found Geoffrey of Monmouth to be the author of *The History of the Kings of Britain* (*Historia Regum Britanniae*)—a purported history that is also seminal in the formation of the Arthurian legends. It was, for a long time, taken seriously as history, but has not been read as a factual work for centuries now. The work was originally split into twelve volumes.

I have some ideas about what the dream might mean. It came days after I finally accepted Socrates' idea that artists are not wise but inspired. It also came amidst my concerns that my reading in philosophy is a hopeless Sisyphean task and that the rapid growth in technology will soon render the human soul and all that matters to me obsolete.

There is something quixotic and hopeful about the dream. It also reminds me somewhat of the formula I put in some song lyrics a while back:

> You have underestimated
> What you wanted to forget:
> Nature, history, nation.

A PARTIAL LIST OF SNUGGLY BOOKS